LET'S
1 PE

CW00393269

Dear Frazer,

It's been a joy, a privilege
and a pleasure serving with you
on Exec this year.
May you always rejoice because of
the coming of the salvation, even
though suffering may come now
May your life be to God's glory
as you continue to grow in his
grace more and more.
'Prepare your mind for action'.
With the love of Christ,
Mark   23.02.06

Let's Study

1 PETER

William W. Harrell, Jr.

THE BANNER OF TRUTH TRUST

THE BANNER OF TRUTH TRUST
3 Murrayfield Road, Edinburgh EH12 6EL, UK
P.O. Box 621, Carlisle, PA 17013, USA

*

© William W. Harrell, Jr. 2004
First Published 2004
ISBN 0 85151 868 0

*

*

Typeset in 11/12.5 pt Ehrhardt MT at the
Banner of Truth Trust, Edinburgh

Printed in Great Britain by
Bell & Bain Ltd.,
Glasgow

TO DEBRA
MY HELPMEET,
MY BELOVED AND MY FRIEND

Contents

Publisher's Preface

*L*et's *Study 1 Peter* is part of a series of books which explain and apply the message of Scripture. The series is designed to meet a specific and important need in the church. While not technical commentaries, the volumes comment on the text of a biblical book; and, without being merely lists of practical applications, they are concerned with the ways in which the teaching of Scripture can affect and transform our lives today. Understanding the Bible's message and applying its teaching are the aims.

Like other volumes in the series, *Let's Study 1 Peter* seeks to combine explanation and application. Its concern is to be helpful to ordinary Christian people by encouraging them to understand the message of the Bible and apply it to their own lives. The reader in view is not the person who is interested in all the detailed questions which fascinate the scholar, although behind the writing of each study lies an appreciation for careful and detailed scholarship. The aim is exposition of Scripture written in the language of a friend, seated alongside you with an open Bible.

Let's Study 1 Peter is designed to be used in various contexts. It can be used simply as an aid for individual Bible study. Some may find it helpful to use in their devotions with husband or wife, or to read in the context of the whole family.

In order to make these studies more useful, not only for individual use but also for group study in Sunday School classes and home, church or college, study guide material will be found on pp. 157–74. Sometimes we come away frustrated rather than helped by group discussions. Frequently that is because we have been encouraged to discuss a passage of Scripture which we do not understand very well in the first place. Understanding must

[ix]

always be the foundation for enriching discussion and for thoughtful, practical application. Thus, in addition to the exposition of 1 Peter, the additional material provides questions to encourage personal thought and study, or to be used as discussion starters. The Group Study Guide divides the material into thirteen sections and provides direction for leading and participating in group study and discussion.

Introduction

Simon Peter, in his earlier life, was an uneducated fisherman from Galilee. He was naturally bold, but brittle. We know of him only because he was called by Jesus to be his disciple. The Gospels show him to be a bold leader – impetuous, boastful, and yet also cowardly. He reaches heights of theological insight when he confesses Jesus to be the Christ, the Son of God (*Matt.* 16:16); he falls to his deepest point when he denies Jesus three times, being afraid to be associated with the God-Man who was heading for the cross (*Matt.* 26:69–75).

We do well to consider some introductory matters before we turn our attention to a detailed and systematic study of this letter. Our understanding of these general matters will help us to understand better the needs of the recipients of the letter and the themes Peter presents while addressing those needs. Our increased understanding will enable us to apply the wonderful truths taught to ourselves.

AUTHOR AND PENMAN

Until the advent of modern, critical scholarship, the church was in agreement that the author of this letter was Peter, the fisherman from Galilee, and the outspoken leader of the disciples of Jesus. Modern critics, however, have challenged this view. They observe that the Greek language in which the letter was written is much too fine to have been penned by an unlettered fisherman. Furthermore, they contend that there is no evidence that Peter was ever in the region where the believers addressed in this letter were located.

In response to these challenges we may observe several things. Firstly, Peter himself appears to tell us that although he is the author of the letter, Silvanus was the penman (*1 Pet.* 5:12). The substance, therefore, comes from the apostle, the fine linguistic style from his secretary. Silvanus (also known as Silas) was a co-labourer with Paul (*Acts* 15:40–41). We may gather, from a comparison of 2 Thessalonians 1:1 with 2 Thessalonians 3:16–18, that Silvanus was a practised penman, having written some of Paul's dictated letters to which the apostle added his own hand-written greeting.

As for the allegation that Peter never visited the area in which the believers addressed in this letter resided, there is no evidence that he did not visit them. We know that Peter travelled outside Jerusalem. From Galatians 2:11 we know he visited Antioch, and we further know that he eventually ministered at Rome. Yet, even if he never had visited them, if personal acquaintance with a people was necessary for an apostle to write a letter of encouragement to them, then Paul would not have written his masterful theological treatise to the church at Rome – a church he never visited (*Rom.* 1: 8–15) until after his arrest, trial, and appeal to Caesar (*Acts* 28: 16–20).

RECIPIENTS AND ROME

The original recipients of this letter are mentioned in its first verse. Peter was writing to believers in north-eastern Asia Minor. It is interesting to note that the apostle Paul, early in his missionary career, was forbidden by the Holy Spirit to enter that area (*Acts* 16:6–7). We do not know how the gospel reached the provinces named here. Yet, through some messenger, the Word of life came to these people, and churches, more or less well organized, resulted. Our saving God has his way of reaching his people, though the human instruments through whom he does so may escape our notice.

These provinces were not in any strategic or vital region of the Roman Empire. It does not follow from this that the believers scattered throughout them were insignificant to God. Worldly position and power do not impress our Lord or his most faithful servants, but divine attention and aid are certainly given in response to the plight of God's people, wherever they dwell.

DEEDS AND DOCTRINE

It is highly likely that Peter was the source for Mark's Gospel (see *Let's Study Mark*, p. xiv), as well as the author of this letter. A common source for these two writings should produce some mutually reinforcing themes between the Gospel and the epistle. We do find such connections when we compare Mark and 1 Peter. In general, the Gospel presents to us the deeds of Jesus, while the epistle expounds and applies the doctrine of our Lord. Yet, the doctrine is ever practical, presented so as to instruct and empower believers to live holy lives. Actions such as Christ's choosing of Peter and the other disciples, and the substitutionary death of Jesus for the sins of his people, receive treatment not only in Mark's Gospel, but are expounded and their significance applied to God's people in 1 Peter also (compare Mark 1:16–20 with 1 Peter 1:1; 2:9, and Mark 10:45 with 1 Peter 1:18,19).

The most prominent connection between Mark and 1 Peter is that of the relation between holiness and suffering made evident in both the Gospel and the epistle. In the Gospel, the holy Lamb of God suffers for the sins of his people, while in the epistle the purifying design and goal of our suffering for Christ is taught (*1 Pet.* 1:6–9; 4:1,2,12–19). Through Christ's redemptive suffering, believers may and must know that their sufferings do not harm them, but serve for their edification. It is our sinning, not our sufferings, that we are taught to dread. Christ has died to redeem us from the former, and his sufferings have transformed the latter into servants for our good (*Rom.* 8:28).

Outline of 1 Peter

1. OPENING GREETING

1: 1–2: Peter identifies himself and his readers.

2. THE GREATNESS OF SALVATION

1:3–12: Here Peter blesses God, the Author and Giver of salvation. The apostle also describes the gift of salvation itself, informing us that it issues from divine mercy and secures for us a living hope. The inheritance we have in Christ is precious, pure, and protected by God for us, whilst we are protected by God for it through faith. This divine protection is not from trials, but sustains us rather through our trials, unto a final salvation so precious that prophets and even angels have fixed their attention on it through the ages.

3. THE CALL TO CONSECRATED LIVING

1:13–2:12: Peter exhorts believers to fix their attention on Jesus as the one thing necessary. They are to be different from what they were prior to their regeneration. They are to be holy, as God is holy. They are to love God and one another, putting away malice and guile. They are to long for the written Word and are to devote themselves to the Living Word as being themselves living stones of his holy temple.

4. THE CALL TO ORDERLY LIVING

2:13–3:12: Peter lists the proper attitudes to be cultivated and exercised by believers in their civil, social, and domestic relationships.

5. THE CALL TO ENDURE SUFFERING

3:13–4:19: Christians are to cultivate peace and avoid trouble by their loving zeal for good works. Yet, though they might be ever so harmless and holy, believers are not to expect to avoid all suffering. Peter is not concerned so much with explaining or even relieving the suffering of believers, as he is with anchoring their faith in the Redeemer, who suffered to save them. Christ suffered for us, we are taught, not so that we might avoid suffering ourselves, but so that we might endure our sufferings rightly, maintaining pure hearts and manifesting loving deeds through the course of our afflictions.

6. THE CALL TO SERVICE AND VIGILANCE

5:1–11: The apostle whom Jesus charged to feed his sheep, here, in turn, reminds elders of their responsibility to pastor the Lord's flock. All true spiritual leadership, however, is to be exercised in humility and to be a manifest example of humility. Such meekness is not the same as weakness. Peter therefore concludes this portion of the letter with a call to vigilance against the devil. Our faith which anchors us to our God and his gracious promises, also acts as our shield against our spiritual foe.

7. CONCLUDING GREETINGS

5:12–14: Peter acknowledges the secretarial service of Silvanus, and testifies that through him he has written true words of divine grace. The apostle then charges his readers to stand resolutely in that grace. He concludes by encouraging them with greetings from members of the church at Rome, stimulating them to show their mutual love, and assuring them of peace in Christ amidst all their conflicts with the world.

I

A Changed Man Greets Chosen People

Peter, an apostle of Jesus Christ, to those who reside as aliens, scattered throughout Pontus, Galatia, Cappadocia, Asia, and Bithynia, who are chosen²according to the foreknowledge of God the Father, by the sanctifying work of the Spirit, that you may obey Jesus Christ and be sprinkled with His blood: May grace and peace be yours in fullest measure (1 Pet. 1:1–2).

FROM SIMON TO PETER

The first word of this letter contains testimony to the saving, transforming grace of God. That word is *Peter*. It was not the writer's name given him by his parents. His given name was Simon. The name Peter, meaning *rock*, was given to Simon by Jesus after he had testified that Jesus was the Christ, the Son of the living God (*Matt.* 16:15–18). The natural man, Simon, was changed into a new creature by the redeeming grace of God in Christ.

He who had been self-reliant and headstrong, whose boasts of his courage and commitment to his Lord melted as he denied Jesus three times, was made, by the restoring grace of God, to live up to the new name given to him by Christ. After his restoration (*John* 21), he who had dreaded and feared suffering, even having gone so far as to offer satanic counsel to Jesus that he should avoid the cross (*Matt.* 16:21–23), was changed into a rock of fearless faithfulness. After Pentecost, this rock of fidelity despised the threats of those who would punish him for preaching Christ (*Acts* 4:18–20), and slept in prison on the night before his own appointed execution with the trusting comfort of a child (*Acts* 12:6). This man, changed by the grace of God from one who feared suffering to one who faced it as more than conqueror, and seeing his afflictions as servants for the refinement of his faith, was the perfect man to write to those believers in Christ in the provinces mentioned who were also suffering.

Peter was suited to his task not only by his vital experience of saving grace. He was also called and commissioned by Christ to be an apostle; a man sent by God with an authoritative message. He therefore wrote to these suffering believers giving them not only his personal testimony of victorious faith, but delivering to them also, and to us, infallible teaching from the risen, victorious Christ. Peter, as an apostle, was serving as the messenger of the holy Son of God, by whose incarnation, perfect life, atoning death, and justifying resurrection, both he and those whom he addressed in this letter were released from sin's bondage into the glorious liberty of the sons of God. All readers of this letter may rely with utter confidence upon the truth, wisdom, love, and power of its contents, because the ultimate source of the letter is the Lord himself.

PERSECUTED BUT PRECIOUS

Those who received this letter can be viewed with respect to their condition and with respect to their position. As far as their condition was concerned, they resided in relatively insignificant areas of the Roman Empire. We gather also from the content of this letter, that they were suffering some measure of persecution (1:6,7; 2:20; 3:14; 4:1, 12–19). Their condition, therefore, was somewhat low and miserable. However, there was so much more to their lives than they perceived with their senses.

With striking effectiveness, Peter reminds them of this by referring to them as a people chosen by God. That divine election made them no longer of the world, though they remained in it. The rejection they were experiencing from the world - their alienation from their fellow-citizens - resulted, ultimately, not from their neighbours' hatred and persecution. God had made them to be aliens in this cursed world by his calling them out of it to be fellow-citizens in the eternal city of God (*Eph.* 2: 19–22). He graciously chose them to be redeemed from sin, death, and hell, and brought them as adopted children into the kingdom of his glorious love.

The apostle John writes in Revelation about his sufferings for the faith on the island of Patmos. He also testifies that by his faith he dwelt, even on Patmos, in the Spirit (*Rev.* 1:9–10). In the same way, these believers lived in two worlds, as do all believers. They lived in the world of men, dead in sin, but they were themselves made alive in Christ. They had to live out their new life amongst fallen humanity in a cursed world, but they were delivered from the dominion of their sin, and were called to sanctification, or holy separation from the world, by the Holy Spirit of God who indwelt and empowered them. In short, they were in, but not of, the world, and were inheritors of a glorious kingdom. Their high status resulted not from their own will or worthiness, but rather from the electing, fore-loving grace of God the Father. Nor were they beholden to an earthly Caesar or to their unbelieving neighbours for their lives and welfare. They were set apart by the Holy Spirit that they might live by, and for, the Christ who had died to redeem them. They had one Master, namely, their gracious, good Shepherd, who had laid down his life for them.

THE BEST AND FULLEST BLESSING

Upon those so loved by God, Peter pronounces the blessing of God's grace and peace. He is not simply expressing a pious wish, but actually conferring upon them the substantial blessing of the Lord. This letter is full of God's grace, declaring what God has done for his people, and what he provides for them in Christ. The abundance of that blessing is alluded to by the words *in fullest measure*. No Christian should ever think that he has received poor or partial blessing from his Redeemer. Every believer has received every spiritual blessing there is to be had in Christ (*Eph.* 1:3).

There is rich, heavenly manna upon which the faith of believing souls may feed, resulting in their having peace which passes understanding. That peace is not a tranquillity in this world, for Jesus never promised his disciples a pilgrimage without conflicts (*John* 14:27; 16:33). Nor is that peace primarily a matter of calm feelings and serene outlook. Rather, it is an objective peace with God, resulting from a justifying faith, which inspires in us a triumphant rejoicing, even in tribulation (*Rom.* 5:1–5).

2

Blessing the Blessed

Blessed be the God and Father of our Lord Jesus Christ, who according to His great mercy has caused us to be born again to a living hope through the resurrection of Jesus Christ from the dead, ⁴ to obtain an inheritance which is imperishable and undefiled and will not fade away, reserved in heaven for you, ⁵ who are protected by the power of God through faith for a salvation ready to be revealed in the last time (1 Pet. 1:3–5).

Peter was a fisherman who was made a fisher of men by Jesus. As such, this apostle does not serve bait or give crumbs of consolation to his suffering readers. Instead, he launches into a rich doxology, blessing God for the great blessing he has poured upon his people. By lifting the focus of these suffering believers from their painful earthly condition, he not only reminds them of their true blessing, but he feeds their souls upon the liberating power of that truth. As they are lifted to a contemplation of their blessed God, they are made to realize, as we are, that whatever believers may suffer for Christ's sake, it is not worthy to be compared with the glorious blessing conferred upon them by God in Christ (*Rom.* 8:18).

THE BLESSED GOD

Peter pronounces God to be blessed. The basic meaning of the word translated, *blessed*, is to speak well of a person or thing. Thus, Peter speaks well of the God of salvation, for God is worthy of all praise in all that he is and in all that he does. The praiseworthiness of God is most apparent in his having given his only begotten Son for the redemption of poor sinners. This infinitely costly gift, and the resulting relationship it has established between God and his chosen people, is captured in the designation of God as the God and Father of our Lord Jesus Christ. Prior to the incarnation of the Son of God, his perfect life and his saving work, all people were related to God as rebellious creatures of their Creator. The blessedness of God is seen in his creation of a world and of mankind that were very good. However, the full measure of God's blessedness is gloriously manifested in the saving of sinners by the Son of God. This salvation is so glorious, that they are no longer mere creatures of God, and sinful, guilty, rebellious creatures at that, but are rather adopted sons of God, greatly loved and abundantly provided for by him as children of a loving heavenly Father.

Jesus had taught Peter and the other disciples about this blessedness of God when establishing a new relationship between himself and his people. After his resurrection and prior to his ascension, our Lord proclaimed to his disciples, *I ascend to My Father and your Father, and My God and your God* (*John* 20:17). With those words, the intimate relationship between God and his people wrought by the costly, atoning work of Jesus is made clear. The primary relationship that believers now have with God is filial. We are his sons, he is our Father. The cost was great because the love of God is immeasurably great.

The Puritan, Thomas Goodwin, remarked in one of his writings that Jesus died for us in order to make us his friends, though he could have made new friends for himself so much more cheaply. Similarly, God gave his infinitely precious, only begotten Son to have us as his sons, when he could have justly blotted us all out and made new sons for himself in a much less costly way. It is this amazing truth which causes the Lord's people to bless him, to speak well of him, to praise and thank him in all things, even amidst their sufferings.

THE MOTIVE OF GOD

God is not only the source of all blessing, but he has also given inconceivable blessing to his chosen people in Christ. Peter makes clear to us what motivated God in blessing us so greatly. It was not that God found worthiness or loveliness in any of his people. Nor was the Lord prompted to assist those who were struggling to save themselves. The divine motive in the accomplishment and application of salvation is sheer mercy. It is by the exercise of his gracious compassion that the Lord deposits a loveliness in his people in whom he could discover no loveliness. It is the love of God that makes us to love him and to love one another. Thus, we learn that the loving and merciful motivation of God is the ultimate ground upon which our salvation rests.

The mercy of God is magnificent. There is nothing small or cheap about it. Sin has rendered us without hope except in God's mercy. Because our sin is great, God's mercy is great, far greater than our sin. The magnitude of God's mercy is beyond our reckoning, and so we should ever think of it as far surpassing any need we have or affliction we may suffer in this cursed world.

THE BLESSING OF GOD

The mercy of God is more than gracious and compassionate sentiment. God's mercy prompted him to action. The blessed God has conferred his richest blessing upon those who did not deserve the least of his mercies. The blessing of God is manifold as well as magnificent. It gives life to men dead in sin, and provides hope for those caught in the hopeless bondage of sin. It also makes provision for every grace that is required from the very beginning of new life in Christ to the perfection of that life in glory.

The first aspect of the blessing of God which believers experience is their regeneration. God has given believers new life in Christ. No man is worthy of this new life, nor can any man achieve it. It is God who has caused us to be born again. We who were dead in sin have been made alive by God in Christ (*Eph.* 2:4, 5). Salvation is not a matter of corrupt corpses being outwardly refined. Rather, it involves a radical change. The dead are regenerated, and everything about them is new. They have a new status before God (justification), a new relationship to God (adoption), and a new destiny (glorification). They have new appetites, perceptions, and power, as well as new relationships and responsibilities.

The glorious consummation of this new life is apprehended by hope. Peter calls it a living hope. We who have been made alive by God in Christ find that we have a real and substantial joy set before us. Our hope is no perishing delusion, as were whatever hopes we had prior to our regeneration. We are not sustained by the husks of this cursed world, or by the vanities of our wishful thinking. Rather, we have a great and glorious hope that enlivens us amidst the most threatening of circumstances.

Our living hope is grounded in and issues from our Lord Jesus Christ. The believers to whom Peter writes are therefore taught that they do not live by, and should not place their hope in Nero, but rather they live by and should hope in the God-Man who has loved them and given himself for them. Their hope was in One who had triumphed over sin, death, and judgment for them. It was not their persecuting enemies, but their victorious Lord who would have the determining say in their lives, as he does in ours. This is why Peter includes the precious and prevailing name of Jesus Christ four times within these few opening verses of his letter.

INHERITANCE AND INHERITORS

This living hope of believers is further described by Peter as an inheritance. The term reminds us that we do not earn or manufacture our estate in glory. Rather, it is given to us, conferred upon us by the death of the divine testator (*Heb.* 9:13–16). Of this inheritance, Peter notes three qualities. There are many more qualities to our heavenly inheritance, but the three Peter mentions are major ones and representative of all other qualities. We should note too that the apostle uses negatives to express these qualities; he says that our inheritance is not perishable, not defiled, and not fading. This tells us that our inheritance is unlike anything we have experienced in this cursed world, where all is corrupt and perishing. The use of these negatives also emphasizes that the nature of our inheritance is essentially far beyond our conceptual powers. It is easier for Peter to say what it is not, than to say what it is. The fullness of that glorious preparation that God has made for us has not, and cannot, enter into the minds even of inspired men (*1 Cor.* 2:9).

Peter informs us that our inheritance is imperishable. It cannot die, be lost, be stolen, be rotted, or be ruined. He further says that our inheritance is undefiled. It is pure and pristine. It is not spoiled, used, marred, or corrupted in any way. Finally, he tells us that our inheritance will not fade away. It will never diminish in vitality, value, or satisfying virtue. The delight and wonder it will inspire in us will never decrease.

This precious inheritance is beyond the destructive power of wicked men and devils. It is reserved in heaven by the almighty power of God for its rightful recipients. Our inheritance is not only preserved by God for us, but we are protected by God through all hazards until we finally and fully possess it. The chosen people of God are protected by two distinguishable but inseparable elements. The first element is nothing less than the almighty power of God. Our Lord can afford to scatter us as aliens in the world, because we are, by his protecting power, secured from all harm. We are, as Jesus said, in the Father's hand, and no one can snatch us out of his hand (*John* 10:27–30). The second element of our preservation is faith – the means by which God's protective power is engaged. By faith, we are not merely survivors of the attacks of hostile men and devils in this world, we are more than conquerors over all such threatening things (*Rom.* 8:35-39).

The suffering believers to whom Peter wrote were well aware of their need of protection. We may be less aware of our need, but that does not mean that it is any the less. We live out our new lives in an old, cursed world which is hostile to God and to the ways, ordinances, and people of God. The work which his great mercy began, will not fail to be completed by the arm of his strength. The salvation we have begun to experience is a sure and finished work of God. Its glorious fullness is complete and is now reserved for us until our course is run. Then the fullness of divine blessing, this great salvation, will be at last revealed to us. Then we shall declare that though it was wonderfully described to us in this life in Scripture and by the sermons and writings of godly men, the half was not told us. Then all remembrance of our alienation and scattering and suffering in this world shall be swallowed up in the joy of the best wine, which our God always reserves until last.

3

Refinement and Results

In this you greatly rejoice, even though now for a little while, if necessary, you have been distressed by various trials, [7] that the proof of your faith, being more precious than gold which is perishable, even though tested by fire, may be found to result in praise and glory and honor at the revelation of Jesus Christ; [8] and though you have not seen Him, you love Him, and though you do not see Him now, but believe in Him, you greatly rejoice with joy inexpressible and full of glory, [9] obtaining as the outcome of your faith the salvation of your souls (1 Pet. 1:6–9).

Peter had heard Jesus bequeath his peace to his people (*John* 16:33). Yet, from what Peter writes in this letter regarding the suffering of believers, we may well conclude that its recipients were enjoying little, if any, peace. Jesus also told his people that they would have tribulation in the world (in the same verse). The apostle of Jesus elaborates on these two propositions in this passage. He speaks of the security of believers in Christ, and also of their suffering in the world. Peter further teaches that these two realities are not unconnected.

Jesus recognized the tension between the peace his people have in him, and the tribulation they endure in the world, and he resolved that tension by his own victory on the cross. He alluded to this when he said, *I have overcome the world.* Similarly, Peter declares that the saints' security and suffering are connected by the wise and loving purpose of God. The sufferings of the faithful are divinely ordained tests, designed not to destroy them, but to sanctify them fully and triumphantly.

[9]

REDEMPTIVE RICHES REVIEWED

Peter began this letter by acknowledging first the temporal condition of his readers. They were living in the world as dispersed exiles (verse 1). To that acknowledgment he added another and higher reality, namely, that they were chosen by God for salvation. This great privilege of salvation serves as the alpha and omega – the beginning and end – of his readers' experience of suffering. Their trials are encompassed within the potent triumph of their salvation. Accordingly, Peter begins verse 6 with the words, *In this you greatly rejoice;* he would have his readers review the riches of their redemption.

The blessings of God's grace and the resultant peace we have with the Lord should be grounds for our rejoicing amidst the most severe trials. The new life we have in Christ, the living inheritance preserved for us, while we are divinely protected through faith for it, are great and precious realities for every believer. These things more than compensate for our sufferings (*Rom.* 8:18). We do well, therefore, to maintain a consistent grasp upon these glorious realities, letting their consoling power cast a light upon our grim suffering and lifting us, as they lifted Paul and Silas to sing joyful praises to God from their dungeon (*Acts* 16:25). For the believer, suffering is not the only reality. It is endured within a blessed context that should be enjoyed exceedingly. The faithful do not simply survive their sufferings, but they have cause to rejoice in them and through them.

REALITY OF SUFFERING

The afflictions of believers can be painful and perplexing. They seem to contradict what Peter said in verse 5 about being guarded by the power of God. But that divine protection operates through the child of God as he exercises his faith. The reality of the sufferings of the righteous is not something that faith denies. The painful and obvious reality we face is something that faith acknowledges. Abraham, for example, acknowledged the virtually dead condition of his aged body; but his faith also acknowledged and rested assuredly in the power of the God who had promised him a son (*Rom.* 4:18–21).

Peter, with understanding and sympathy, takes note of the distress his readers were suffering as a result of their numerous and varied trials. The word in verse 6 translated *trials* has also the connotation of temptation. By Peter's use of it, he admits that adverse experiences can tempt believers to have hard and bitter thoughts about the God who has allowed so many afflictions to come upon them.

The faithful may begin by honestly facing the fact of afflictions, but they do not end their consideration there. By faith, we lay hold of the consoling plans and purposes of God in our suffering. Peter therefore does not stop with his sympathetic acknowledgement of his readers' trials. He goes on to interpret those trials in the context of the sure and living hope of believers. This hope, apprehended by faith, cuts present sufferings down to size. For example, Peter speaks of his readers being afflicted now, and not forever. There will be an end to their trials. He also characterizes the duration of the saints' afflictions as being only for a little while. By these expressions, the apostle is not trivializing the afflictions of believers so much as magnifying the divine consolation to be attained through divinely ordained trials. Paul does the same thing when he speaks of our slight momentary affliction producing for us an eternal weight of glory (*2 Cor.* 4:17–18).

By faith, we perceive not only the obvious and undeniable reality of suffering, but also so much more that is not obvious. It is this unapparent dimension, perceived only by faith, that is determinative for us. Part of this determining reality, apprehended by faith, is that our trials are only of temporary duration. However long they may last, they will come to an end. Another determining factor is the sovereign superintendence of God over all our trials.

The afflictions of the children of God do not result from chance or from a lapse in divine vigilance or power. As God granted Satan permission to afflict Job (*Job* 1:12; 2:6), so the Lord, for wise, holy, and loving reasons, ordains the course of our afflictions. This reality is alluded to in Peter's phrase, *if necessary* (verse 6). That necessity issues not from unavoidable circumstances, but rather from the sovereign will of God. The divine will guarantees that our pains produce glorious fruit.

Peter knew this from his own experience. Jesus told him that Satan had demanded permission to sift the boastful disciple like wheat

(*Luke* 22:31–32). We know that sifting is a purifying act, whereas Satan is determined to corrupt and destroy the Lord's people. What made Satan's vicious temptations into a purifying test was God's sovereign ordaining and gracious superintending of the trials, mediated through the prayers of Jesus. God uses the sin of men and devils sinlessly to sanctify his people. Our Redeemer also ever lives to make such intercession for us (*Heb.* 7:25).

REJOICING IN REFINEMENT

It is in our Lord's sovereign ordaining and governing of our afflictions, not in the afflictions themselves, that we rejoice. We look to the loving and wise hand of our heavenly Father, applying the refining trials to us, and to the glorious fruit of righteousness that is imparted to us through such testing afflictions. In these things we exult (*Rom.* 5:1–5; *Heb.* 12:4–11). However, it is only by exercising our faith that we can rightly perceive and submit to God and his blessed purposes for us through our trials. This fact makes the purifying and strengthening of our faith to be a matter of great importance. Peter, therefore, teaches us more specifically what God accomplishes through our trials, namely, a refinement of our faith.

When a goldsmith thrusts gold into the fire, he does so not with the intention of destroying the gold. The fire will not, in fact, hurt the gold, but it will burn off imbedded impurities and thus serve to enhance the value of the precious metal. So it is with our sufferings. Our heavenly Father employs the furnace of affliction not to ruin, but to refine the faith of his people. The faith of Job emerged from his trials more pure and strong than ever. As Daniel's friends emerged from their fiery furnace with only their bindings burned away, so believers emerge from their trials having lost only their fears and doubts in the consuming flames of affliction.

The genuine character of faith emerges and is enhanced through trials. If Daniel's friends, by their faith, did not fear the threats of Nebuchadnezzar before they were thrown into the fiery furnace, they certainly did not fear the power of that king, nor anything in creation, after they emerged unscathed from the flames, having been preserved by the shield of their faith. Similarly, the disciples of Jesus, whose weak faith revealed itself on the stormy sea, viewed their Lord with a deeper and stronger faith after they had gone through the storm and had entered into the peace of the Lord's making (*Mark* 4:35–41).

As our faith grows pure and strong through its exercise in trials, we rejoice to an increasingly greater degree. Our faith enables us to stand as more than conquerors through all that could possibly come against us (*Rom.* 8:31–39). We have the greatest cause for rejoicing in the fruit of proven faith.

RESULTS OF REFINEMENT

Peter tells us not only of God's purpose in our trials, but also of the divinely cultivated products of our trials. The refinement our faith undergoes results in God's glory and in our great good.

1. *The glory of God:* Peter does not clearly specify in verse 7 who gives the praise, glory, and honour he mentions, but we can hardly believe other than that these things are offered by the faithful to the God who has brought them safely through all their earthly trials. God is glorified through our sanctified sufferings. By faith refined through trials, we learn increasingly to perceive the wisdom, power, and love of God in sustaining and sanctifying us in all our tribulations. Accordingly, we praise him for his wise and loving employment of our trials for our good (*Rom.* 8:28). We also honour him for his sovereign and almighty sustaining power. In all, we ascribe glory to God for his incomprehensible plans, his inscrutable will, and his immeasurable love – all of which we grasp, not exhaustively, but more clearly, deeply, and firmly through a tried and tested faith.

The full and perfect praise, glory, and honour of God, however, will be rendered only on the final day. Peter speaks of that day as *the revelation of Jesus Christ*. Paul uses the same term (*2 Thess.* 1:7). We usually speak of the coming or return of Jesus. Yet the apostolic designations of our Lord's coming as a revelation emphasize that Jesus is even now, in time, more near at hand and apprehendable by faith than we might realize. On that last day, however, we shall behold him fully and forever. On that eternal day, which renders all of our earthly days as but a momentary vapour, we shall see all things, not as they appear, but as they truly are. Then shall burst forth from us not one word of complaint, not one question regarding God's wisdom, love and power. Rather, at the beatific sight of our Redeemer, with all our tears wiped away, we shall offer ceaseless praise, glory, honour, and thanks to our God (*Rev.* 4:11; 5:12–13).

In the midst of our sufferings the scriptural emphasis, that God's care for us throughout our earthly pilgrimage will be finally and perfectly vindicated, is not elusive, distant, or irrelevant. This certain conclusion to our course of trials should fortify us to begin now, by faith, that employment of praising God which will on the final day of revelation be our eternal occupation and pleasure.

2. *Our great good:* The glory of God is not maintained at the expense of the welfare and lasting happiness of his people. We are most blessed as our God acts for his highest glory. Men and holy angels would have cause to glorify God were he to enable us adroitly to avoid trial and affliction. Yet, there is even greater cause for us to glorify God when he plunges us into trials and causes them to serve for our good rather than for our harm.

The good we derive through trials is mentioned by Peter in verses 8 and 9. Amidst his trials, the believer does not, with embittered desperation, curse God and die. Rather, the faithful are enabled to cast themselves more vitally upon the loving care and blessed communion of their risen Saviour. We do not see Jesus now, but we do see the things we suffer. But faith quickens us in afflictions to ask for, seek after, and find the deep, deep love of Jesus. We love him who stands with us in the flames of our trials. We experience deeper and sweeter intimacy with him as we share in the fellowship of his sufferings (*Phil.* 3:10).

Not only is the believer's love for Jesus quickened in the furnace of affliction, but the joy of the faithful grows to inexpressible character and dimension as well. What we see tells us that we have cause to dread and grieve over the things we suffer. But by the exercise of our faith in Jesus, we find that we have a shield that both quenches destructive darts thrown at us by wicked men and devils, and also transforms those very missiles into fuel for our joy (*Eph.* 6:16).

A fireman may have confidence in his protective suit during a fire drill. Yet when that suit preserves him in the middle of a raging inferno, he is then filled with deeper gratitude for its shielding qualities, and he joyfully and gratefully extols its virtues. In the same way, believers do not love or rejoice in Jesus less because he preserves us in our trials. We love him all the more, and rejoice in him to the glory of his Name as he brings us through the fires of testing, making us better than we were before.

The final outcome of our trial-tested faith is the salvation of our souls. By this, Peter means the full and perfect salvation which we inherit on the final day. The character of that salvation must be so indescribably great that when it becomes fully ours its glorious wonder will swallow up any pain and perplexity we may have endured in the course of our earthly trials. Our current sufferings – no matter how varied and awful they may be, no matter how long they may last – are not worthy of comparison with the glory and felicity of that magnificent salvation. This is our highest, everlasting good, which is enhanced, not diminished, by the trial and triumph of our faith.

4

Salvation's Man and Message

As to this salvation, the prophets who prophesied of the grace that would come to you made careful search and inquiry, [11] seeking to know what person or time the Spirit of Christ within them was indicating as He predicted the sufferings of Christ and the glories to follow. [12] It was revealed to them that they were not serving themselves, but you, in these things which now have been announced to you through those who preached the gospel to you by the Holy Spirit sent from heaven – things into which angels long to look (1 Pet. 1:10–12).

Peter moves on from considering the testing of the faith of suffering believers (verses 6–9) to a consideration of the object of their faith. He has acknowledged that his readers had never seen Jesus as he had (verse 8). But they were not at any disadvantage because of that, and neither are we. By faith we lay hold of the Saviour and of salvation in him. Peter saw Jesus, having followed him as one of the twelve disciples for three years. However, as the Gospels make clear, the fisherman turned disciple said and did many foolish and faithless things as he walked with Jesus. It was not his sight of, but rather his faith in Jesus as the saving Son of God that truly blessed Peter (*Matt.* 16:15–17).

The suffering believers to whom Peter wrote were encouraged by the apostle to understand the value of their faith. Even more were they encouraged to appreciate the supreme value and vital nature of the salvation which they grasped by their faith. Peter therefore now writes of the saving Man, the Christ, the Son of God, and of the message of his salvation. The work of the Saviour is not the rare possession of those few who had seen, heard, and touched Jesus. It is a gift of God, graciously designed to be transmitted to others. Those laying hold of Christ and his salvation by faith, possess something thoroughly prepared and purposely presented to them by God.

THE WORK OF THE PROPHETS

Peter informs us of the precious and potent character of the salvation possessed by believers by faith, when he reminds us that the work of salvation was predicted over the course of centuries by the prophets of God. What they saw, spoke, and wrote by inspiration of God, was essentially a message of saving grace. They beheld, in various ways and to various degrees, differing views of the Lamb of God and his saving work. Though the prophets were numerous and lived in different places and at different times in Israel's history, they all conveyed the same essential message. They declared that by God's gracious determination and design a costly redemption of sinners from the bondage and misery of their sin had been undertaken and would be accomplished. This was to be done not by man earning his salvation, but by the holy and beloved Son of God providing that salvation.

The prophets were not casual or careless in their reception or declaration of their precious message. What they saw and spoke was not something they fabricated. It was not something new in their day, but was a message revealed through the Lord's inspired servants over centuries. Their prophecies did not result from their own mistaken conjectures or poor and erroneous understanding. Rather, we are told, the prophets made careful search into the messages they received from the Lord. If they were uncertain about any aspect of their burden, they made inquiry so that they might better understand and more faithfully declare the words of God (*Dan.* 10:12; 12:8–9).

The fact that so many prophets of God should declare over so many centuries the gracious salvation of God, and that they took the greatest care to maintain fidelity to the revealed mind and will of God, should assure us that our Saviour and his salvation are absolutely reliable. Those prophets who beheld and declared God's redemption before its accomplishment in our world, display to us a consensus that the salvation the Lord promised through them, and would provide through his Son, warrants supremely careful consideration and application.

WHO? WHEN? AND WHAT WORK OF SALVATION?

The prophets made careful search into the person of the Saviour, the timing of his saving work, and the character of the work he would accomplish. They were not led in their search and in their subsequent prophecies by their own curiosity or quest for speculative knowledge. Rather, they were borne along by the Holy Spirit (*2 Pet.* 1:21), whom Peter here calls the Spirit of Christ, because it has always been, as it now is and ever will be, the Spirit's mission to glorify Christ (*John* 16:13–14).

Therefore, the prophets ever pointed to the Man of God's choosing, the personal Saviour of God's people. They were not philosophers or mystics, propounding principles gathered by their own reflections. They knew and consistently pointed to the truth that the message of salvation concerns at its heart a Man. Jesus brought this truth into clearest focus when he said to his opponents: *You search the Scriptures, because you think that in them you have eternal life; and it is these that bear witness of Me* (*John* 5:39). He was emphasizing the same truth when he said that Abraham saw his day and rejoiced (*John* 8:56), and when he informed the two disciples on the road to Emmaus that the person of Christ is to be found in all the Scriptures (*Luke* 24:27).

The prophets also inquired into the timing of the coming of the Christ to accomplish the redemption of which they prophesied. Again, their inquiry was not speculative but sanctifying. For them the event of Christ's coming took priority over the time. He who brought the fullness of salvation, they rightly reckoned, would come in the fullness of time, or, we might say, at the perfect time. Thus, the prophets spoke of the time of Messiah's coming as the last days (*Isa.* 2:2; *Mic.* 4:1). By this we should understand that the incarnation, atoning work, and ascension of the Son of God formed the final divine accomplishing action in redemptive history, prior to the return of Jesus at the end of time. What an immense privilege the scattered aliens to whom Peter wrote had, that they lived in the last days, when God had accomplished salvation in Jesus. What a privilege we have to live in the light and certainty that the work of redemption is finished.

In addition to their careful search into the Person and time of salvation, the prophets were by God's Holy Spirit enabled to understand and predict the nature of the Saviour's work. His would be a career of sufferings. From the humiliating circumstances of his birth, through the obscurity of his growth, the contradiction of his enemies, leading to his arrest, trial, mockings, beatings and crucifixion, and to his death, and burial in the tomb of another man – the life and death of our Saviour were filled with sufferings. However, he bore those afflictions willingly and in order that he might attain glories that would more than compensate for them all. As Jesus himself said, it was necessary for the Christ to suffer all that he did and thereafter to enter into his glory (*Luke* 24:26). By his submitting to the sufferings incumbent upon his office of Redeemer of sinful men, he attained a name above every name in earth or heaven (*Phil.* 2:8-11). This is the way the Master went. We, his servants, must follow in the same way, entering into the Kingdom of God through many tribulations (*Acts* 14:22).

THE WORD FOR OUR WELFARE

The Son of God came not to be served, but to serve, giving his life as a ransom for many (*Mark* 10:45). His servants – the prophets, the apostles, and the preachers of his Word – also do not seek to be served, but to serve those chosen by God for salvation. Therefore Peter declares that the prophets served not themselves, satisfying their own personal interests, as they prophesied regarding the Christ and his saving work. They were serving the believers to whom Peter wrote, those of his own day and of all days thereafter. We are in a most privileged position, being the recipients of everything of which the prophets wrote concerning the Christ. They prophesied in part, but we, by taking together all that they wrote, have a clearer apprehension of the whole.

It was not only the prophets of God over many ages who declared their prophetic burdens for our sake. The apostles of Jesus also, who with the prophets form the foundation of the church (*Eph.* 2:20), declared through their preaching and New Testament writings, the fullness of Christ and his saving work. They, too, served for our sake. Through their testimony regarding the Person and work of Christ, we have God's fullest and final Word (*Heb.* 1:1–2). As the Spirit of Christ inspired the prophets, he also inspired the apostles, so that they also proclaimed the unique, precious, and prevailing redemption wrought by Jesus Christ.

The scattered aliens to whom Peter wrote surely felt impoverished as they considered themselves from the standpoint of this world. Peter raises their perspective, and ours, so that they and we might recognize that God has lavished his very best upon us. Our heavenly Father has employed prophets over many centuries and apostles in New Testament times, to serve us in a way that should overwhelm with grace and glory all that grieves us in this world. Great men have been raised up by God to serve us. They have spoken and written for our sakes, pointing us to the Lamb of God, the suffering servant of the Lord, who has come and has accomplished for us a work of such grace, grandeur, and glory, that angels are amazed and gripped, and are filled with holy wonder that we sinful humans should be so richly blessed.

5

Called to Conform to God

Therefore, gird your minds for action, keep sober in spirit, fix your hope completely on the grace to be brought to you at the revelation of Jesus Christ. [14] As obedient children, do not be conformed to the former lusts which were yours in your ignorance, [15] but like the Holy One who called you, be holy yourselves also in all your behavior; [16] because it is written, 'You shall be holy, for I am holy' (1 Pet. 1:13–16).

The Gospels show Peter as the most active of the disciples of Jesus. If Peter was the source for Mark's Gospel, then we should not be surprised to find so much action, as we do, in that account of the life and ministry of Jesus. Nor should we be surprised to find that in this letter of Peter's the apostle quickly moves from doctrine to deeds. This transition is not the result of the carnal rashness and faithless impetuosity that characterized much of Peter's action in the Gospels. Instead, Peter, by inspiration of God's Holy Spirit working through his uniquely practical personality, resolutely begins to build upon the doctrinal foundation he has laid. This fisher of men is determined to make captive the minds, hearts, and actions of those to whom he ministers. He not only declares to his readers a comforting heavenly doctrine, but challenges them to holy living. He does this by directing his readers to attitudes and actions that are consecrated to their saving God.

PREPARED MINDS

The call Peter issues to his readers in verses 13–16 is a call to nothing less than complete conformity to the character of God. Their minds, their appetites, their aspirations, their actions, are all to be brought captive to Christ. The first thing Peter calls for is the girding of the mind. We may recall how Peter, in the Gospel accounts, tended to act first and then think. Here he more correctly calls for holy action to be informed and guided by right thinking.

The image Peter employs is vivid and instructive. It alludes to the instructions God gave his people on the eve of their exodus from Egypt. They were to eat the Passover lamb with girded loins, sandals on their feet, and staff in hand (*Exod.* 12:11). In other words, when the people of God partake of the saving provision of God, they are to be prepared for empowerment to walk in freedom and holiness.

We gird our minds when we direct our thoughts consistently to the mercies of God in Christ. By this our minds are transformed (*Rom.* 12:1–2). We also gird our minds when we store them, not with the distractions and trinkets of this world, but with the liberating truth of God's Word.

That liberation wrought by a faithful laying hold of the truth leads to righteous actions. Remember that Peter was writing to scattered, suffering saints who were treated by their fellow-citizens as aliens to be scorned and abused. The trying circumstances in which Peter's readers lived would have surely pressured them into feeling sorely abandoned. Furthermore, they would have been greatly tempted to act on those feelings, venting their despair in words if not actions. This was the temptation for Asaph in Psalm 73 when he beheld the wicked living in luxurious ease while the righteous suffered. Peter calls his readers to gather up their distracted thoughts, focusing them on the truth of God in Christ, and to act accordingly. They were to think in accordance with the truth God had revealed in his Word, and then to be prepared to act on the basis of its enlightening and liberating power.

CONTROLLED APPETITES

In addition to his exhortation to gird the mind, Peter calls his readers to maintain sober thinking and living habits. The girded mind keeps us from sinful distraction; sober living keeps us from sinful dissipation. When we are amidst painful, trying circumstances, as were the believers to whom Peter wrote, we will find ourselves tempted to blunt the edge of our afflictions by intoxicating ourselves. We may do this through drink or drugs. We may also intoxicate ourselves by excessive entertainment or through any form of self-indulgence. In his second letter, Peter mentions Lot's trials and commends him, calling him righteous, which he was by God's grace (*2 Pet.* 2:7–9). However, Lot, after having been graciously delivered from Sodom by God, gave in to temptation. In a cave near Zoar, he allowed himself to become drunk, no doubt feeling that the wine offered to him by his daughters was necessary to give him relief from the pain of having lost his wife and home in God's judgment upon Sodom. Yet, far from finding relief, Lot fell into disgraceful sin; a sin which produced bitter consequences for God's people for ages to come, in the form of the Moabites and Ammorites (*Gen.* 19:30–38).

In contrast to those seeking escape from their misery through various forms of dissipation, we have the example of Jesus at the cross, refusing the mind-dulling mixture of wine and myrrh (*Mark* 15:23). When a man is dissipated, he can neither think clearly nor act in a consecrated fashion. The sober man, possessing all his faculties in proper working order, can not only feel keenly the pain of a trying situation, but can also grasp the provision of God by which he is empowered to be more than conqueror in all that he endures.

FIXED HOPE

The Christian is not only directed to have a sober mind. He is also directed to have a certain focus and direction to his thoughts. As far as his current trials are concerned, he is by faith to appropriate the liberating and empowering truth of God. He is thereby well-equipped to stand and serve as more than conqueror in time. Furthermore, those redeemed by Christ and regenerated by God's Holy Spirit have an ultimate hope which, when rightly grasped by faith, sustains them in time just as much as it compensates them inconceivably in eternity. Accordingly, Peter exhorts his readers to fix their hope upon the final revelation of Christ.

The object of our hope is the grace of God, which we currently have and by which we stand and serve our Lord. Yet that grace is but a pledge, a down payment, a token of a fullness which far outweighs whatever sufferings we may now be called to endure (*Rom.* 8:18). Grace is what the Puritans rightly called *young glory*. It is that grace culminating in glory which is to be the focus of our hope. The scattered and suffering believers to whom Peter wrote were not to place any hope in their persecutors tiring of their attacks or softening in their opposition to the servants of Christ. Believers are never to hope in natural endowments, attainments, or circumstances. Neither are they to hope for any mercy from the world. Rather, they are directed to hope completely in the Lord (*Psa.* 118:9).

The attitude of this hope is to be one of fixed certainty. The word translated *completely* in verse 13 literally means *perfectly*. Thus, we are to have a determined and unchangeable focus, not on the perishing things of this time or world, but on heavenly things, where Christ is, seated at the right hand of God (*Col.* 3:1–3). When our faith fixes upon the final revelation of our Redeeming Lord, we are fortified to endure the trials of our pilgrimage. Dissipation offers only a delusory and temporary relief from the pains of our afflictions. Hope fixed upon the final, glorious vindication which shall be ours in Christ affords us prevailing strength and enduring security, so that we are actually sanctified through our trials, rather than being shamefully overcome by them.

CULTIVATED HOLINESS

The Apostle John instructs us with the encouraging truth that when we fix our hope on Christ, we become like him who is the object of our hope (*1 John* 3:3). This is so because true hope, fixed on Christ, begets in us a desire and determination to be like Christ, and, more specifically, to become closer now to what we shall be forever in the final day when we shall see the face our Saviour and reign with him in glory (*Rev.* 22:4–5). It is to this life of conformity to our holy God that Peter calls us in verses 14–16. The call contains both a negative and a positive dimension. We are not to conform to what we were prior to our regeneration, and we are positively to cultivate that holiness which is characteristic of our heavenly Father.

Peter begins with the negative. Believers are, by their faith, new creatures in Christ (*2 Cor.* 5:17). However, we are not perfected at our regeneration; nor do we automatically grow to perfection. As new creatures, we have our minds, emotions, and wills set free from the dominion of sin, but not from its remains. Therefore, we are exhorted by God's Word and enabled by his Spirit to will and to do righteousness (*Phil.* 2:12–13). We are enlightened by this Word to know what moral purity is, to understand righteous action and holy being. We are given an appetite – a hunger and thirst – for righteousness (*Matt.* 5:6), and this, coupled with the exhortation to be holy and to do righteous deeds, leads us to grow in holiness. Such growth necessarily involves our resistance and refusal to be conformed, not only to the spiritually dead and perishing world (*1 John* 2:15–17), but also to what we ourselves were when we were dead in our trespasses and sins (*Eph.* 2:1–3).

Peter in particular calls for our non-conformity with the former lusts of our ignorance. By this, he means our ignorance of God, and of the beauty of his holiness and the sweetness of his love. He means also the ignorance of God's merciful provision for our salvation in Christ. In such ignorance, all the unregenerate live, move, and have their being. They grope about in darkness, not having the light of God's Word. They are urged on by irrational and impure passions which inflame hunger but never lead to its satisfaction. From such ignorance and misery we, who are in Christ, have been set free. Yet, we must determine that, by God's gracious enabling, we shall never lapse into being the wretches we were before our conversion to Christ.

It is not enough however to resolve never to lapse into unregenerate patterns of thinking and living. The house must not merely be cleared of its old demons, but it must be filled with godliness. Therefore, Peter goes on to exhort his readers to put on their new and true selves. This involves a conformity to the holy character of the One whose redemption and effectual calling released us from our actual sins, as well as from the dominion of sin. By Christ, we have been separated from sin and set apart for God. Such separation is the essence of holiness. It is the cultivation of the purity and moral excellence which exist essentially and perfectly, in God. This cultivation of holiness may be new to us, and it calls for expending energy and effort. Yet, for the redeemed it becomes increasingly natural and delightful, since they are conforming themselves to their heavenly Father who has lovingly adopted them in Christ.

The pattern and power for our cultivation of holiness are both found in God. Holiness is determined by who God is and by what he does as an expression of his being. The testimonies, commandments, and teachings of his Word, not our feelings, personal tastes, the dictates of society, or the traditions of men, define holiness. The commitment, promise, and provision of God supply the power for our attainment of holiness. He who is holy has not only instructed us to be like him, but enables us by his calling to be holy.

6

Called to Reverence

And if you address as Father the One who impartially judges according to each man's work, conduct yourselves in fear during the time of your stay upon earth; [18] knowing that you were not redeemed with perishable things like silver or gold from your futile way of life inherited from your forefathers, [19] but with precious blood, as of a lamb unblemished and spotless, the blood of Christ. [20] For He was foreknown before the foundation of the world, but has appeared in these last times for the sake of you [21] who through Him are believers in God, who raised Him from the dead and gave Him glory, so that your faith and hope are in God (1 Pet.1:17–21).

The grace culminating in glory on which we are to fix our hope (verse 13) is not a divine indulgence of our sins. The last thing our partaking of the saving grace of God in Christ should make us is casual as regards our living the Christian life. Therefore, Peter exhorts his readers to holy living (verses 14–15). Our response to such an exhortation is a serious matter, involving far more than a dutiful endeavour to conform our actions to a righteous standard. The God who calls us to be holy, as he is holy, is more to us than a living standard of holiness. He is our loving, heavenly Father, the universal Judge of men and angels, and the Redeemer of his people. Because we are related to our holy God in these ways, we should be most careful and reverent in our attitude toward, and service for, him.

THE ONE FEAR NECESSARY

Peter adds further incentives to our commitment to holy living when he reminds us that the God who has saved us and whom we serve is our Father, Judge, and Redeemer. These relationships with God in which believers find themselves should reckon supremely in the estimation of the children of the Lord. They form the nexus of the one thing necessary in our lives, and call for an attitude of reverence from us.

Our familiarity with the Lord, and our luxuriating in his gracious love, should banish all fears from our lives except for the one fear necessary. That is why Peter calls his readers to conduct themselves in fear throughout their earthly lives. He is issuing a call for believers to have reverence for the living God. The suffering ones to whom Peter was writing would have found themselves surrounded by fearful circumstances. There is evidence in this letter that they were suffering for their faith, and they may have therefore feared for their jobs, their liberties, their lives. Peter calls upon those saints to have a proper reverence for their God, whereby they would learn not to fear suffering so much as to dread sinning against, and grieving, their heavenly Father.

Believers are to conduct themselves in godly fear. By this we are to understand that our highest regard must constantly be for God, and neither for men nor for the circumstances surrounding us, whether they be enticing or intimidating. We are to hear and heed one Master in our lives. As the eyes of servants look to their master for his direction, protection, and provision, so we should be fixed with reverent attention upon our God (*Psa.* 123:2). As the three disciples on the Mount of Transfiguration were told by the voice of God to hear his beloved Son only (*Matt.* 17:5), so we are to concern ourselves neither with the plans and ploys of our enemies, nor with the fair invitations of our friends, but only with the wise and loving will and glorious honour of God.

The duration of this godly fear is intimated when Peter says that it should be our guiding attitude throughout our stay or sojourn. By this he means that the fear of God should be maintained by us throughout our pilgrimage in this life, beset as we are in it by wicked men and devils. The fear of God should not come upon us in occasional episodes, but should burn steadily within us throughout the course of our walk in this life. We become casual with God to our detriment. But if he is our one holy fear, we shall be set free from all other fears in heaven, hell, or earth, in time or eternity.

INCENTIVES FOR REVERENT LIVING

The apostle gives several incentives to encourage our commitment to reverent and holy living. All of these incentives issue from the relationship that obtains between God and his people. Who our God is in relation to us and what he has done for us should fill us with such loving gratitude that we commit ourselves to live for his pleasure and glory.

1. God is our Father. The first incentive Peter gives for our holy living is the relationship in which we stand to God. He is our Father; we are his adopted children. We stand in this relation to God because of the great love with which he has loved us (*1 John* 3:1). He has loved us, and has given his only begotten Son in order that through the Son's redeeming work, the Father might have us as his adopted sons. Because he so loved us, we love him (*1 John* 4:19). He has adopted us, conferring his name upon us when we were baptized in the name of the Father, Son, and Holy Spirit. Therefore, we should desire to please and honour him.

A right understanding of the biblical doctrine of adoption will never lead us into a heedless manner of living. The spirit of adoption we have received enables us to cry to our Father in terms most familiar and intimate (*Rom.* 8:15). However, that spirit does not prompt us to be presumptuous, but rather, grateful and careful. It gives us a supreme love for our Father by which we dread disobeying and grieving him.

2. God is the Universal Judge. The next incentive Peter gives for inspiring reverence in the children of God is the reminder that God is the Judge of all the earth. By his omniscience, God knows all we do, think, say, and intend. He needs no prosecutor or witnesses to present evidence to him. As Judge, he is not simply an all-knowing observer; he calls to account every deed done by all men. The standard by which he judges is perfect righteousness, and he is an impartial and incorruptible Judge.

Peter, in reminding us that our Father is the Judge of all, is not in any way contradicting the believer's assurance of salvation. He is not denying what Jesus says about believers not coming into judgment, but passing out of death into life (*John* 5:24). Nor is he overturning the glorious truth expressed by Paul when he wrote that there is no condemnation for those in Christ Jesus (*Rom.* 8:1). The very fact that even though we do sin, we have a righteous Advocate with the Father (*1 John* 2:1, 2), makes us more, not less, determined to fear God and resist all temptation to sin. The fact that the Judge is our Father, who acquits us on account of our Redeemer's work, should fill us with joy, but also with reverence for such a majestic mercy that has triumphed over justice (*Psa.* 2:11; *James* 2:13).

Indeed, Jesus himself teaches us to pray to our Father in heaven that his will be done on earth as in heaven (*Matt.* 6:10). Such a petition hardly gives us licence to live in such a way that we would be contradicting our Father's revealed will.

3. *God is our Redeemer*. God is not only our Father and the Judge of all men. He has also planned our redemption in the counsels of eternity and accomplished our redemption in Christ in the fullness of time (*Eph.* 1:3–12). Peter touches on this incentive for our holy living in verses 18 and 19. The apostle reminds us particularly of the cost God bore in our redemption.

Our gratitude would be rightly due to anyone who paid our monetary debts, or who provided money to pay a ransom to our captors. The greater the payment, the deeper and more lasting should be our gratitude. Jesus illustrates this principle in his parable of a money-lender forgiving two debtors, one having owed much, the other, little (*Luke* 7:40–47). Yet, we sinners have not been redeemed with money, but with the shed blood of the Son of God. Nor have we been redeemed from monetary debt or some form of captivity, but rather from our sins against the holy God who is Judge of all men.

Sinners naturally suppress the truth that they are rebels against God and guilty before the sovereign Judge (*Rom.* 1:18). They live as though they themselves were gods. But both their suppressions and pretensions are futile, having no basis in reality, even though this is how men live naturally and how they teach their children to live by both precept and example. From such vanity and misery and ever compounding guilt before God, believers were redeemed by a gift of God's own giving.

The price God bore for our redemption was no less than that of the giving of his Son as an atoning sacrifice for the sins of his people. Peter uses the adjectives, *unblemished* and *spotless* to describe the character of the life given for the sins of God's people. The first word, *unblemished,* was often used to describe the Old Testament sacrifices; but the second word, *spotless*, was not. Christ, the sacrificial lamb given to atone for our sins is hereby shown to be the perfect substance of salvation, of which the animals sacrificed under the ceremonial law were but shadows and imperfect copies. The infinitely precious and perfect life of the Son of Man was poured out for the sake of vile, guilty, and corrupt sinners. The price of our redemption was infinite, and its cost was undertaken graciously by God. How could we, who have received this gift, live in any way other than the way of godly fear and gratitude?

4. *God is the source and goal of salvation.* In verses 20 and 21 we are reminded that our redemption was not the result of some divine after-thought, but issued from the eternal counsels of God. The source of our salvation, therefore, is not in our desire or need, but in God's inscrutable mercy. Peter tells us that before the foundation of the world, God planned and purposed to make a new creation. The new creation would issue from his eternal Son's incarnation, perfect life, and atoning death. The Father's seal of acceptance of the sacrificial work of his Son was manifested by his raising Jesus from the dead, and exalting him to the place of his right hand in glory.

The redemptive work of God in Christ, having been accomplished, was consequently applied to sinners by the Holy Spirit. In this way, those who were dead in their trespasses and sins were made alive together with Christ by God's grace (*Eph.* 2:1–9).

When Peter mentions the foreknowledge of God, he informs us not only that the price of our redemption was great, but also that the divine planning that determined the payment of our redemption was extensive – more extensive than the whole of time. Yet, these vast and ultimately incomprehensible considerations are made powerfully personal when Peter writes that all was predetermined and accomplished by God, *for the sake of you*. This holy God, to whom we are to conform ourselves, and before whom we are to live reverently, has done all things for our good (*Rom.* 8:28). Thus, we may place all of our faith and hope in him through Christ, and we shall never find ourselves to be disappointed (*1 Pet.* 2:6). Indeed, it is in God that we must place all our faith and hope. Then and only then can we live as sojourners in this world, having our affections set upon that heavenly glory to which we are destined, and living now in ever growing conformity to our holy Father, who loved us, and his holy Son, who gave himself for us, and the Holy Spirit, who now indwells and sanctifies us.

7

Called to Brotherly Love

Since you have in obedience to the truth purified your souls for a sincere love of the brethren, fervently love one another from the heart, ²³ for you have been born again not of seed which is perishable but imperishable, that is, through the living and abiding word of God. ²⁴ For, 'All flesh is like grass, and all its glory like the flower of grass. The grass withers, and the flower falls off, ²⁵ but the word of the Lord abides forever.' And this is the word which was preached to you (1 Pet. 1:22–25).

The Christian life is full of paradoxes. We are told in God's Word, for example, to set our minds on heavenly things, rather than on the things of this earthly life (*Col.* 3:1–4). Yet, paradoxically, those people who are most heavenly-minded are the ones who are of most earthly good. Thus the Apostle Paul, who wrote that believers should be heavenly-minded and was certainly so himself, showed throughout the shipwreck episode of Acts 27 and 28, that he was eminently practical. Another paradox in the Christian life has to do with the commandment for us to love our God with all our heart (*Matt.* 22:37). It would seem, if we loved God with our whole being, that we would have no love to give to our fellow-men. Yet, by the command and enabling power of God, those who love the Lord completely also love others as no one else can.

THE SECOND GREAT COMMANDMENT

In this passage Peter draws out the connection between loving the Lord and loving one another. From his instructions regarding holy living (verses 13–21), he proceeds to teach us that our holy living breeds loving, happy relationships with our brethren. The connection between these two is not coincidental, but causative. When the lawyer asked Jesus to articulate the great commandment in the law (*Matt.* 22:36), he was expecting our Lord to identify one supremely important commandment. Jesus did so by summing up the first four of the Ten Commandments – all of which have to do with our duty towards God – by saying that we are to love God with all of our hearts. However, Jesus did not stop there. He went on to speak of a second great commandment, that could be distinguished but not separated from the first great commandment. We are to love our neighbour as ourselves as an inevitable fruit of our loving the Lord above all.

The supreme love we owe to God was touched upon in verses 17 to 21, where Peter wrote of God's sacrificial and immeasurable love for us. Therefore, in verses 22 to 25 the apostle calls for the fruit of loving God to be manifested in love for our brethren. In this call, Peter is following the lead of Jesus, who told his disciples that if they loved God, they must also love one another (*John* 15:9–17). Other apostles, such as Paul (*Eph.* 4:7–16), and John (*1 John* 4:7–21) consistently bind the second great commandment to the first great commandment. What the Lord and his apostles have so joined together, we may not tear asunder.

HOW WE ARE TO LOVE OTHERS

Paul instructs us to speak the truth in love (*Eph.* 4:15). Likewise, Peter joins together the truth of God and love when he reminds us that our obedience to the truth of God is to draw from us a love for our fellow-believers. It is of the nature of the purifying work done in the heart by the enlightening and liberating truth of God that we, being freed increasingly from the sin that alienates us from God and from our fellow-men, should be empowered to love both our heavenly Father and our brethren in Christ.

Peter does not simply call his readers to the exercise of such brotherly love, he defines several important aspects of that love. By giving us details of how we are to love one another in Christ, we are directed to a fuller understanding of the character of the love we should have for others. If we find ourselves lacking in any aspect of this love, we should prayerfully ask God, who is love, to lead us to a fuller, deeper, and more vibrant love of the brethren.

Peter touches on four aspects that should characterize how we love our fellow believers:

1. *Purely.* Our love should not issue from selfish, carnal passion. Rather, we who have been cleansed by the washing of regeneration (*Titus* 3:5), have been freed from the dominion of sin which alienates us from both God and man. Consequently, we are directed to exercise love towards one another in Christ with our sin - the great impediment to such love - having been substantially removed. The residue of our sin is also to be removed progressively by the process of mortification. The blight that made us self-absorbed has been, and is being, removed, so that we who have the mind of Christ look out lovingly for the interests of other members of the body of Christ (*Phil.* 2:1–4).

From purified souls issues love that is pure, undefiled, and undefiling. Our love should be holy, and should encourage our beloved brethren in their cultivation of holiness.

2. *Sincerely.* The love we are to have for our brethren is not to be feigned or put on hypocritically. It is rather to be deep and genuine. Our loving actions should not be dutifully performed rites of civility, but should flow from the warmly compassionate attitude characteristic of those who are children of the God of love.

It is true that Scripture speaks of our putting on a heart of loving compassion (*Col.* 3:12–14). This does not mean, however, that for the sake of politeness we are to act lovingly whether we feel loving or not. Instead, we are called to don, inwardly as well as outwardly, our new and true selves in Christ (*Col.* 3:10), and to resist the loveless momentum of our old, sinful natures.

3. *Fervently.* Our love for our brethren is not to be weak in its strength or minimal in its quantity. The standard of our love for other members of the body of Christ is found in the source of that love. Our blessed Redeemer commands us to love one another even as he has loved us (*John* 13:34). Therefore, our love should be warm, zealous, strong, and sacrificial. As the Son of God loved us and gave

himself for us (*Gal.* 2:20), so we should fervently love our brethren to the point that we unsparingly give of our time, energies, and substance.

4. *Thoroughly*. Our love is to be from the heart. This would seem to be synonymous with saying that we are to love sincerely. However, while the words, *from the heart*, do imply sincerity and integrity in our love, they also mean more than that. We are, as it were, to treasure our brethren in our hearts. We are not to love them with sincerity only when we are face to face with them. Rather, we are to keep our brethren in our hearts and prayers perpetually. This would involve, for example, reflecting upon the precious members of the church whether known directly or by report, thinking kindly, compassionately, and prayerfully of them regularly. It should be obvious from this that we are instructed to guard our hearts from growing cold and disinterested towards them, to guard our minds from thinking hard and bitter thoughts about them, and to guard our tongues from speaking destructively to or of them.

SEED AND SUSTENANCE OF LOVE

Peter's call for his readers to love their brethren in Christ is not simply the expression of an empty and powerless moral platitude. His appeal is made to those who have been made new creatures in Christ, and who are well equipped by God to love one another. He speaks therefore of his readers' regeneration, the instrumental means of their new life, and he contrasts this new life with the old.

1. *New birth*. When Peter calls his readers to exercise brotherly love, he expects them to hear and heed the call because of who they are. Thus he begins verse 23 by giving the enabling reason upon which his call for brotherly love is based: *for you have been born again*. Peter is addressing a people who had been regenerated by God's Holy Spirit. They had been effectually called by the Spirit from their state of death in sin to a state of new life in Christ. As new creatures in Christ, they had a new status through being justified and adopted by God; they had new desires as children of their heavenly Father; they had a new direction for their lives from God's Word; and they

were filled by the indwelling Spirit with new power to know, do, and delight in the will of God (*Phil.* 2:12–13).

The scattered aliens to whom Peter wrote had been wrought upon by the Spirit of the living God, who is love. Therefore, the apostle has a confident expectation that his call for them to love one another will not go unheeded, but will fall on the hearing ears, transformed minds, and loving hearts of new creatures in Christ.

2. *The seed of new life.* The Spirit of God is the divine agent bringing men to new birth in Christ. The instrumental agent of that new birth is the Word of God. The Spirit of God uses God's Scriptures to bring people out of death and into life. Therefore Peter speaks of the Word explicitly as the seed of the new birth, and refers to the Spirit implicitly, as the effective agent of that new birth. If we think of the Parable of the Sower (*Mark* 4:1-20), we recall that Jesus spoke of the seed as being the Word (*Mark* 4:14). The varying conditions of the soils represent the hearts of men of differing states of receptivity to the Word. The only lastingly productive soil, is called the good soil (Mark 4:20), and though not mentioned in the parable, we know from elsewhere in the Word that it is the Spirit of God who works on men's hearts to make them truly receptive of the Word.

The image of the Word of God as precious and imperishable seed alerts us to the fact that the Word is not merely information which men can take or leave, but a growing and enduring potency. The Word is the power of God unto salvation for all who believe (*Rom.* 1:16). Peter refers in particular to the preached Word (verse 25), which serves as the instrumental source and sustaining power of our new life in Christ. Accordingly, the Word is not perishable but imperishable, living and abiding. Heaven and earth will pass away, but the Word of God will ever remain a living force, giving holy and loving life to believers.

3. *New life and old contrasted.* The living and abiding character of the Word of God is in great contrast to the transitory nature of fallen man's life and experience. Peter draws out this contrast between the new life in Christ and the old life from which believers have been redeemed. Unregenerate man with his mental, social, and

material constructions seems impressive and enduring, until that point in time when the Word of the Lord is spoken. The situation then is rather like when the disciples of Jesus marvelled over the grandeur of the temple, only to be told by their Master that not one stone would be left upon another (*Mark* 13:1,2). The Word of God reveals man's lost state, his guilt before God, his perishing hopes, and his growing misery. Peter quotes from Isaiah 40:6–8, where the voice of the Lord declares by the prophet the transitory state of fallen man, and, in complete contrast, the life-giving and abiding character of God's Word.

Why does Peter give this contrast at this point in his letter? He does so to make clear to his readers that they are what they eat. If we feed on the husks of this world, we shall grow lifeless, hopeless, and loveless. If we feed on the preaching of God's Word, we shall be enlightened with truth and empowered with love. The scattered aliens to whom Peter wrote were probably tempted to feel that their sufferings would never end. To give in to such feelings would render them hopeless and cynical. Peter counters these dark feelings with the facts of God's Word. By that Word preached to them, the believers to whom Peter wrote had become new creatures, children of their heavenly Father, and brothers and sisters together in Christ. By the Word, they were called to live the truth in love. Such living is the mature fruit of regeneration. It should show in our lives, no matter what transient circumstances may for a little while be afflicting us.

8

The Right Spiritual Diet

Therefore, putting aside all malice and all guile and hypocrisy
and envy and all slander, ² like newborn babes, long for the pure
milk of the word, that by it you may grow in respect to salvation,
³ if you have tasted the kindness of the Lord (1 Pet. 2:1–3).

Peter has compared the preaching of the Word of God to a sowing
of precious seed; it brings us to the new birth in Christ. However,
the Word does not only begin our new life, it also sustains it,
nourishing us, feeding the new nature, so that we grow and develop
as God intends. Salvation is not a pill we swallow once, then wait
for it automatically to release its potencies; nor is it an insurance
policy that we sign, then wait for its cover to be activated when the
need arises. Scripture portrays salvation as a pilgrimage (*Psa.*
119:54), as a race (*Heb.* 12:1), as a walk (*Isa.* 40:31; *Rom.* 6:4), and as
a life (*John* 5:24); growth and progress are always taking place.
Therefore, the apostle, in the opening verses of this second chapter,
issues another practical exhortation. He urges believers to hunger
for the Word that has served to give them new life in Christ so that
they might grow to maturity in the Lord (*Col.* 1:28).

THINGS NOT IMPEDING SPIRITUAL GROWTH

With respect to the suffering of those to whom Peter wrote, it is
almost as remarkable for us to note what he does not list as being
impediments to spiritual growth as that which he does list. As far as
obstacles to spiritual growth are concerned, Peter is significantly
silent over such things as suffering, poverty, deprivation, poor living

conditions, or persecution. He is silent regarding these things because, in fact, there is nothing in our circumstances which can impede our growth in the grace and knowledge of Christ. We may think that the church suffers when she lacks civil rights or monetary means to carry on her mission. We may feel that our sickness, injury, or lack of celebrity status, can disable us from living lives pleasing to the Lord and testifying to his saving grace. However, the Bible teaches us that none of these circumstantial things can in themselves harm us. On the contrary, God uses them for our good (*Rom.* 8:28), and makes us to be more than conquerors in all things (*Rom.* 8:37).

It is not our circumstances that impede our spiritual growth, but rather our sins. We can serve God's glory and grow in sanctification as readily in poverty and suffering as did Job. We can testify to Christ's saving work as powerfully in a prison as in a palace, just as Paul and Silas demonstrated in the prison at Philippi (*Acts* 16:19–34). Peter therefore disregards the harsh living conditions of his readers.

IMPEDIMENTS TO SPIRITUAL GROWTH

What Peter does emphasize in this exhortation to spiritual growth is a list of sins that his readers should mortify. Their spiritual nourishment would not only be retarded by the contradictory effects of the sins listed, but it is most difficult, if not impossible, to profit from a study of the Word with these vices mentioned in verse 1 being cherished in the heart.

Peter lists five sins to be mortified. The list is not exhaustive, but representative of those sins most antithetical to the holy love enjoined in 1:13-25, and most destructive of relationships between brethren called to love one another.

1. *Malice.* The antithesis of love is hatred. Malice is closely related to hatred, in that it is an attitude in which one actively wills ill toward another. The malicious person desires and determines to harm others.

The word translated *malice* in this verse is actually more general in the original Greek. Its root is the word, *bad*, and means badness or wickedness. As it is used here, it implies the desire for bad, evil, or wicked things to happen to others. It is shocking to think that believers who have been loved by God and dealt with so mercifully by the Judge of all the earth, should have within themselves malice towards others. Yet, if we examine our attitudes closely, we may well find this sin within us militating against our Lord's commandment that we love one another.

2. *Guile.* Believers are called to be pure (1:22) and to have integrity in their dealings with others. Guile is the opposite of purity and integrity. It is a cloak of cunning, slyness, and craftiness, donned as a protecting shield by the guilty. Guile is the resort of those whose position is guilty and inferior. They must operate under cover of deceit and darkness.

Believers are called to walk in the light. Our dealings are to be open and honest, letting our *yes* be *yes* and our *no* be *no*. It is through such straight dealings issuing from pure hearts that progress is made in sanctification, and holy love is enabled to flourish amongst brethren.

Peter writes that all malice and all guile are to be laid aside. This means that we are to take a ruthless and radical approach to these vices. Not even a mild form of malice or necessary resort to guile must be tolerated by the children of God's love and light.

3. *Hypocrisy.* The word translated, *hypocrisy*, as well as the two following vices of envy and slander, are all found in the plural in the original Greek. Perhaps this is because these sins are conceived of by Peter as having more concrete expression in overt actions. Hypocrisy is certainly related to guile. It is one of the tools of guile's nefarious trade. Hypocrisy is antithetical to speaking the truth in love. The hypocrite either lies to protect or to promote himself; he feigns love when, in order to hurt the hearer, he tells the truth that he knows will be painful. Satan speaks the truth when he accuses the brethren, yet he does not do so in love, nor does he tell the whole truth.

4. *Envy.* With malice, we intend another's harm; with envy, we begrudge another's good. Envy is the attitude of resentment towards the blessing of others. It is a low and mean attitude. At times envy

gives us a desire to misappropriate to ourselves the good things that rightly belong to others. In its lowest form, envy would lead us, if possible, simply to deprive others of their blessing without taking it to ourselves, because we do not so much love the blessing as hate the one whom we envy.

5. *Slander*. A primary tool employed to act out envy is slander. By it, men speak lies about others in order to injure them. The aim of slander is the promotion of the slanderer at the expense of the one slandered. It is the antithesis of preferring others in honour, and humbly regarding others in the body of Christ as more important than ourselves (*Phil.* 2:3). Slander is the opposite of that love which covers a multitude of sins (4:8).

Why does Peter select these five sins in particular? Part of the answer is that they are especially contrary to the love we are to cultivate for our brethren (1:22). Another part of the answer is that we do not grow spiritually while we view other believers as competitors whom we must demote by any means so that we may be promoted. There may yet be another part to the answer. Under the pressure of suffering, such as the first readers of this letter endured, we may be strongly tempted to retaliate against our persecutors with malice, guile, hypocrisy, envy, and slander. We may feel that these attitudes and actions are necessary and justified. But Peter identifies them as sins, and as such they neither defeat our enemies nor preserve us, but they defile us and destroy our friendships.

These and related sins are in us, even though we are redeemed in Christ. Therefore, we must identify and mortify them. However, though these sins are in us, they are no longer of us. That is why Peter directs us to lay them aside, as vile garments which may have been essential to us in our guilty poverty, but which no longer have any place in our lives, now that we are children of the King of glory.

TRUE SPIRITUAL NOURISHMENT

1. *How we should hunger.* Peter passes from the necessary but negative work of mortifying residual sins, to the positive matter of feeding

on the Word of God. Nourishment for the redeemed soul is not composed of the vices listed in verse 1, but rather of the true and loving provision of God through his Word.

The apostle begins by emphasizing how we should hunger for the Word. He says we are to long for the ministry of God's Word as newborns long for their mother's milk. We are to hunger and thirst for the Word. We are to delight in our reading of Scripture, and find satisfaction in its proclamation to us by preaching. We are not merely to tolerate it as something forced upon us.

The image of newborn babes also conveys to us the notion of our having a sense of utter need and dependence. We are not to come to God's Word with a critical attitude, but rather with an attitude of humility that comes from the realization that in our highest development as Christians, in our greatest growth in the grace and knowledge of the Lord, we shall still only weakly grasp the full magnitude of God's glorious truth and love. Our highest wisdom is the realization that so long as we see through a glass darkly (*1 Cor.* 13:12), we know only in part and vaguely, as do infants. Far from this knowledge frustrating us, it should comfort and encourage us, knowing that the pains and perplexities that may overwhelm us do not overwhelm our wise, almighty, and loving heavenly Father. Nor will they overwhelm us while we exercise faith now, here below, and their memory will not hurt us when we are perfected in glory.

2. *For what we should hunger.* That for which we are to hunger is the pure milk of the Word. Literally, the expression is: *unadulterated spiritual milk*. The seed of God's Word is also the nourishing milk of the soul. The gospel which was the power of God for our conversion is also the provision of God for our nourishment and growth in grace. As a mother's milk is the best nutrition for her baby, so we are to understand that it is the Word of God that best feeds the spiritual children of the Lord.

We may be tempted to imbibe men's speculations or their efforts at entertainment, but we who are in Christ are not made to subsist on such husks. We must hunger for the one thing necessary, the Word of the Lord, which happily is the one thing that God commands his ministers to preach in the churches of Christ (*2 Tim.* 4:1, 2). Only by hungering for, and feeding with relish upon, the Word of God do we truly grow. The sentimental, sensual, and carnal elements that men endeavour to add to the ministry of the Word, may tickle our ears, entertaining us for a time, but they can never satisfy or edify our souls.

3. *Results of right feeding.* Our right feeding on the Word of God results in our growth in respect to salvation. By this, Peter means that we make vital and valuable progress in the knowledge of the liberating truth, power and love of God in Christ. That believers grow in this way is the will and agenda of God (*1 Thess.* 4:3). It should be our determined goal as well. If it profits a man nothing to gain the whole world and lose his soul, then it can profit those who are redeemed by the Lord nothing to grow in their respectability amongst ungodly men, in their material fortunes, in their intellectual and aesthetic power, while they neglect so great a salvation.

THE INDISPENSABLE CONDITION

In verse 3, Peter adds a condition to his exhortation. All that he has said will make sense only to those truly regenerated in Christ. The apostle's call for the mortification of the sins listed in verse 1, and his urging of his readers to hunger and thirst for the Word of the Lord is regarded by the natural man as foolishness. Yet, for those who have tasted and seen that the Lord is good, kind, wise, and caring, this exhortation is a call to delve more deeply, fully and vitally into the pleasures and joys that God holds in his hand for his children (*Psa.* 16:11). A lack of spiritual appetite indicates a lack of spiritual life. Those hungering most for the Word of the Lord are those who have tasted that he is good (*Psa.* 34:8) and who desire more of that which the Lord delights to give to his children.

9

The Rock of Salvation

*And coming to Him as to a living stone, rejected by men, but
choice and precious in the sight of God, ⁵ you also, as living stones,
are being built up as a spiritual house for a holy priesthood, to
offer up spiritual sacrifices acceptable to God through Jesus
Christ. ⁶ For this is contained in Scripture: 'Behold I lay in Zion
a choice stone, a precious corner stone, and he who believes in
Him shall not be disappointed.' ⁷ This precious value, then, is
for you who believe. But for those who disbelieve, 'The stone
which the builders rejected, this became the very corner stone,'
⁸ and, 'A stone of stumbling and a rock of offense;' for they stumble
because they are disobedient to the word, and to this doom they
were also appointed* (1 Pet. 2:4–8).

When Jesus was tempted by Satan in the wilderness, one of the
temptations our Redeemer resisted was the changing of stones
into bread (*Matt.* 4:3–4). The Son of God certainly had power to
effect such a transformation, but in his office as the Redeemer of
God's people he did not have authority to do so. In verse 4 of our
passage, Peter employs a transformation of imagery.

The apostle had been speaking about food, namely, the milk of
the Word, but at this point he changes his imagery to that of a stone.
Many metaphors are required to describe accurately the multi-
faceted nature of the Saviour's Person and work. Even with such rich
and varied descriptions we shall realize, when we see our Lord face
to face, that not the half has been told us of his glories.

WRITTEN AND LIVING WORD

Peter has exhorted his readers to long for the unadulterated milk of the Word. By this exhortation, he urges us to hunger and thirst for the Scriptures. However at verse 4, Peter's exhortation advances from commending the *written Word* to a commendation of the *living Word*. Consequently, we are led from the principles of Scripture to the Person of Scripture. In our longing for the nourishment of Scripture, we are drawn to the Person of Christ, who is the theme of all Scripture.

The Word of God has Christ as its source, theme, and goal. We must never approach the nourishing Word as though it were merely a collection of truths or a compendium of principles. There is a Man in the sacred book. Jesus told his opponents as much when he said to them that they searched the Scriptures thinking that in them they would find eternal life, but that the Scriptures testified of Christ, and that eternal life issued only from him (*John* 5:39). Jesus again drove this point home to two of his disciples on the Emmaus road. He charged them with being foolish and slow to believe the Scriptures when they doubted his resurrection. Then Jesus showed them how Moses and the prophets all spoke of the atoning sufferings and justifying resurrection of the Christ (*Luke* 24:25–27). Through our feeding on the written Word of God, we should understand that we feed by faith upon the living Saviour. We may distinguish the living Word from the written Word, but we can never rightly separate them.

APPROACHING THE LIVING WORD

Regarding this living Lord of the Word whom we approach, Peter stressed four things:

1. *A living stone*. At Caesarea Philippi, when Peter's faith prompted him to confess that Jesus was the Christ, the Son of the living God, our Lord pronounced the confessing disciple blessed, and changed his name from Simon to Peter, meaning rock (*Matt.* 16:16–18). However, the bedrock upon which salvation is built is Christ, not Peter. Therefore Peter rightly refers to Christ as a living stone. This image conveys to us the truth that our Saviour is stable and solid.

But unlike the lifeless rocks of this world, Jesus is termed a living stone. He is not dead and cold as a stone, though he is solid as one. In addition to our Saviour's strength, he is alive and life-giving. There are caring, loving, wise and sympathetic facets to our living stone. Thus we are to know that we approach One who is both strong and sensitive.

2. *Rejected by men.* The strength, sensitivity, and infinitely precious nature of the rock of our salvation are not seen or accepted by all men. The natural man rejects the Saviour and his redeeming work. Peter therefore candidly admits that those who come to this living stone must reckon with the world's rejection of that stone and of all who rest and rely upon him. Jesus warned his disciples of this, saying that if the world hates them, they must know that it hated him first (*John* 15:18–20). This primal hatred and rejection by the world of the Saviour explains why those looking to Jesus for salvation also experience the same hatred and rejection. The alienated, suffering, scattered believers to whom Peter was writing are thus informed that their sufferings were for and in Christ, and were thus evidences of divine blessing (*Matt.* 5:10–12).

3. *Chosen by God.* In contrast to the rejection of Christ by men, this living stone was, with all care and determination, chosen by God. By this Peter means that, in the counsels of eternity, the Son was chosen by the Father to be what no one or nothing else could be. The Son of God was chosen to be incarnate, thus assuming to himself the nature of man, so that as the Son of Man he could live a perfect life and die an atoning death for man. The Son of God was chosen to save sinners by his sufferings (*Isa.* 53:10–12). It was not a choice that his Father forced upon him, but one that he voluntarily accepted and performed. This living stone was the chosen champion of God's people, standing as David did for Israel against Goliath and the Philistines, and prevailing against all their enemies.

4. *Precious to God.* The living stone to whom we come was not only chosen by God to serve as the Saviour of God's people – he is also a beloved Son. Peter heard the words of the Father on the Mount of Transfiguration: *This is My beloved Son with whom I am well*

pleased; hear Him (*Matt.* 17:5). Though sinful men despise and reject this living rock of salvation, God counts him infinitely precious. The supremely wise and majestically sovereign God is capable of evaluating with truer judgent than fallen, finite man, that which is truly precious. The living God counts as supremely precious this living stone to whom we come, and through our union to Christ by faith, our God regards us also as precious, beloved treasures, no matter what rejection and abuse the world shows to us.

BECOMING LIVING STONES

The living stone to whom we come is unique in his person and work, but he is not a solitary living stone. We who come to him also become living stones, by our union with him. Being stones, we then have enduring stability through time and eternity. We are strengthened and empowered to stand victoriously in the most evil of days (*Eph.* 6:10–18). But we are also living stones. No longer are we dead in our trespasses and sins. We are alive to God (*Rom.* 6:11), and live to love our saving Lord and his people. We are also chosen by God's grace to know and serve the Lord, and are, like his Son, precious in his sight.

The living stone of Christ and the living stones of those who have faith in him are not merely a random assortment of wondrous and vibrant stones. Peter lists, in verse 5, three aspects of what it means to be a living stone in Christ.

1. *Temple incorporation.* Those made living stones in Christ are not independent or randomly scattered entities. The divine hand that cut these stones from the mass of humanity, dead in sin, did so to incorporate them into a building. While it is true that believers grow personally as they feed upon the milk of the Word, they also grow corporately as they assemble together for worship (*Heb.* 10:25) and stimulate and serve one another in Christ (*Phil.* 2:1–4; *Heb.* 10:24). We find a type of this work of building in the history of the construction of Solomon's temple (*1 Kings* 6), and Paul elaborates upon the spiritual reality of the building in Ephesians 2:17–22. What Paul calls a dwelling of God in the Spirit (*Eph.* 2:22), Peter discusses in terms of a spiritual house. Where even two or three believers

gather in the name of Jesus, the Lord is there not only indwelling them individually by his Holy Spirit, but also manifesting himself by the Spirit in their midst (*Matt.* 18:20).

The final and fullest description of the spiritual house of God is found in Revelation 21 and 22. We should know that our highest and most significant place is that station which we possess in the Church – the body and bride of Christ. The scattered aliens to whom Peter wrote needed this comforting truth and we, in these days of great mobility and individualism, need it no less.

2. *Holy priesthood.* We in Christ are being fashioned by God into a spiritual house. But we are living stones, and not lifeless or passive parts of a building. Therefore Peter changes the focus from the building to those working in the building. He informs us that we are a holy priesthood. However wretched and despicable believers may appear to the world or even feel themselves to be, they are holy in the sight of God, and useful in the Lord's service. They have a constant and perpetual calling to minister not only to men in Christ's name, but much more also to God through Christ. This calling does not depend upon believers living in prosperous nations and fine houses. That to which they are called and are enabled to offer to God can be offered up even in the darkest and most dire circumstances.

3. *Spiritual offerings.* We are called by Christ to make disciples of all nations (*Matt.* 28:19–20). Yet that service, with its outward orientation toward men, is not the Christian's only or even primary calling. We may not always be in company with men to whom we can offer the gospel. More often, we are living, working, and serving among a people opposed to the gospel. Such was the case with the original recipients of this letter. Thus Peter reminds us that while the times for speaking to men about God come and go, the times for our serving God in our prayers and praises never depart.

We are to offer God not physical offerings, but spiritual sacrifices. These sacrifices are defined by Paul when he tells us to present ourselves entirely to God, offering up to him our bodies, minds, and souls for his glory, pleasure, and disposing (*Rom.* 12: 1–2). Nothing in heaven, hell, or earth can or should stop us from rendering to God our wills, our hopes and aspirations, our endowments and attainments, our time, energy, and talents, our possessions, friends, and family.

ASSESSING THE LIVING STONE

Peter supports what he has said in verses 4 and 5 by an appeal to Scripture. His use of the stone and building imagery is not the fruit of his own imagination. He has, rather, been drawing out the teaching of Old Testament Scriptures in order to show us how God planned and foretold through the prophets what he had provided for his people in Christ, the rock of salvation.

1. *The assessment of Scripture.* Peter's imagery has been drawn from Scripture. In verse 6, he cites Isaiah 28:16 in order to confirm what he had said about Jesus being the living stone, choice and precious in the sight of God. From this reference, it is clear that God chose the most precious and enduring person possible to accomplish that upon which all of salvation depends. The living stones built upon him are referred to in the second part of the quotation from Isaiah as those who believe in him. By faith, men dead in sin are united to the living stone laid by God as the corner stone of the new creation. Those so united become themselves living stones.

What Peter said about men's rejection of the living stone he now supports by other quotations, from Psalm 118:22 in verse 7, and from Isaiah 8:14 in verse 8. Scripture thus predicted the plans, purposes, and provision of God in choosing his Son to be the precious and perpetual rock of salvation. Scripture also predicted that of which the scattered saints to whom Peter wrote were well aware, namely, that many men reject this precious living cornerstone.

2. *The assessments of faith and unbelief.* These estimations and declarations of God recorded in the Old Testament and reaffirmed by the apostle in this New Testament letter, are seen, understood, and accepted by believers. By faith, men hear and obey the Saviour as he invites them to come to him for rest (*Matt.* 11:28–30). By faith, people rightly perceive the precious value of the cornerstone of salvation, and by faith, they entrust their entire welfare in time and eternity to him. By faith, they stand, and serve for the glory of God,

and despite all the costly sufferings they may have to bear, they testify to having no regrets for their faith in Christ, but only cause for ceaseless praise and thanksgiving to God.

The estimation of this rock of salvation is very different from the perspective of unbelief. Faithless men can and do become respectable and religious. But they are not thereby made living stones, nor do they prize the rock of salvation. The unregenerate leaders of Israel thought they were building a people for the glory of God, even as they were rejecting the foundation of all that would be acceptable to God. To unbelief, Christ crucified is an insult and offence. Unbelievers refuse to acknowledge that their sin is so great, that only the death of the Son of God can save them from its terrible consequences.

But the rejection of unbelievers does not stop Christ from building his Church (*Matt.* 16:18). Those who refuse the living Word and disobey the written Word do not frustrate what God has done and is continuing to do in Christ. Instead, they destroy themselves by their own darkened hearts and rebellious hands. Even in their determined disobedience, they do not rob God of his glory, but work out, rather, in their pride and presumption, their own condemnation – that doom to which God has sovereignly and justly appointed them.

Peter mentions this because believers, scattered and suffering amidst the masses of unbelievers, can be tempted to divert their focus from Christ, and become overly concerned with the agendas of faithless men. The apostle accordingly exhorts his readers to remove their eyes and thoughts from those who are stumbling and rejected by God, and return their faith and affections to Christ, the precious, choice, living rock of salvation.

10

The Chosen People of God

*But you are a chosen race, a royal priesthood, a holy nation, a
people for God's own possession, that you may proclaim the
excellencies of Him who has called you out of darkness into His
marvelous light; [10] for you once were not a people, but now you
are the people of God; you had not received mercy, but now you
have received mercy* (1 Pet. 2:9–10).

However much the world despises Christ, he is the choice and
precious cornerstone of the Church. However contemptuously
the world may treat Christians, they are the chosen, living stones of
the spiritual house of God. Believers are not chosen by God because
they are inherently precious. The exercise of the sovereign and saving
grace of the Lord deposits loveliness in the saints, it does not discover
it in them. This saving election of God bestows a manifold loveliness
upon its recipients, and it is this immensely precious character,
together with its correspondingly high and holy conduct, that Peter
draws out in this passage.

WHAT ELECTION DOES FOR SINNERS

The saving election of God accomplishes many marvellous things
for those who are its objects. Great changes take place in the status,
relationships, appetites, direction, and destiny of those who are
chosen and called by God to inherit salvation. Peter mentions four
such changes in verse 9. They are all corporate rather than personal,
and yet they imply the personal dimension as well. Peter has drawn
all of the four from Scripture, and, had he intended to do so, could

have added other glorious designations of the people of God from the Word. The four aspects the apostle records here have special reference to the needs of his readers.

1. *Chosen race.* The Christians to whom Peter wrote were scattered and were suffering persecution. Their circumstances would easily have suggested to them that they were the scum of the earth, rather than beloved sons of God; trash, not treasure. Yet, in the heart of God, they had been chosen from the mass of humans who were dead in trespasses and sins. They were chosen to be made alive together with Christ (*Eph.* 2:4–5).

Such divine election makes its objects possessors of the highest status and most rich and glorious fellowship. It does not result from any inherent worthiness on the part of its recipients. In fact, those so chosen are lifted from depths of sin, guilt, corruption, and misery as deep as that of other sinners. Moses makes clear that Israel's election by God resulted not from any endowment or attainment they had to commend them to God, but rather from God's free grace (*Deut.* 7:7–8).

While divine election applies to individuals, it finds its highest expression in the corporate relationship that believers have with each other in Christ. Those chosen by God's grace are made new creatures individually, but they are also forged together by love into a community, a family, a body composed of like-chosen new creatures. Thus Peter refers to the scattered ones to whom he writes, not simply as chosen persons, or saved individuals, but rather as a chosen race, of which each member shares in the immeasurable love of God and receives every spiritual blessing in Christ.

2. *Royal priesthood.* The people of God are not only the objects of divine election. They are, by that election, elevated to highest office. In the Old Testament, the offices of priest and king were distinct and separate. The priests held the highest spiritual office, whilst the kings held the highest civil office. Each office was one of great authority and power. No man holding one of those offices was to usurp the prerogatives of the other, as we learn in the case of King Saul when he acted as a priest and offered sacrifice, instead of waiting for Samuel to perform that service (*1 Sam.* 13:8–14). Only in the

person of our blessed Lord Jesus do we find the offices of prophet, priest, and king legitimately combined.

Those in Christ may be considered by the world as being of no account, but, by the gracious exaltation of God in Christ, believers are made into a kingdom of priests (*Rev.* 1:6). As priests, we offer spiritual sacrifices to the Lord (verse 5). With no priestly mediator except for our sympathetic high priest, the Lord Jesus, we offer our lives as living and acceptable sacrifices to God (*Rom.* 12:1). In addition, we reign with our sovereign Lord. By faith we now reign, however imperfectly, over all things as more than conquerors (*Rom.* 8:35-37). In the glory of eternity we shall by sight reign perfectly with Jesus forever (*Rev.* 22:4, 5).

3. *Holy nation.* In Christ, we are not scattered aliens, but fellow-citizens with the saints of God (*Eph.* 2:19). We have mutual rights and responsibilities in the Church that transcend all racial, cultural, and national boundaries. It is said in Scripture that through the exodus led by Moses, a nation was born in a day (*Isa.* 66:8). God forged a multitude of oppressed slaves into a nation when he graciously and mightily released them from Egypt. However, that exodus and creation of a nation was but a shadow and type of the spiritual commonwealth created by God in Christ.

Our national identity in Christ is not limited to time and space, or to those social, economic and national constructs erected by man. Those who are in Christ form a holy nation. And as a holy people they are consecrated, or set apart, from sin and for God. The moral and spiritual excellencies of the Lord's holiness should characterize our individual lives, as well as permeate the body of the Church. Many of our trials and afflictions are sovereignly ordained by God so as to separate us from the sinful mass of men, and from sin itself, and drive us more deeply and vitally into possessing and demonstrating that holiness without which no man will see the Lord (*Heb.* 12:14).

It is said of the Church Father, Basil, that among other bodily afflictions, he suffered from severe headaches. He prayed for their relief, and was answered with a long spell without headaches. During that spell, he experienced an alarming increase in lustful thoughts. He therefore prayed that if the headaches were the means of vanquishing such sinful thoughts, they might return; and they did. Holiness is the charter and constitution of the covenant nation of God.

4. *Prized possession of God.* The world may hate and persecute God's people, but God loves and treasures his children as trophies of his costly, redeeming grace. God takes special care to secure the people he is building into his own dwelling in the Spirit (*Eph.* 2:22). The beauty of holiness that he is forming in them is for his own glory and pleasure. We learn this from Ezekiel's touching account of Jehovah choosing, claiming, and cultivating the wretched Jerusalem to be his own bride (*Ezek.* 16:1–14). Paul speaks of the riches of the glory of God's inheritance in the saints (*Eph.* 1:18). Our God is glorified by, and pleased with, the loving and undistracted devotion of his people, because it is a response to his own unreserved giving of himself in Christ to us in his eternal love. It is also an immense comfort to believers to know that in whatever condition they dwell, their glorious God is pleased to dwell in that condition with them and in them.

WHAT THE ELECT DO

The saving election of God not only changes the character and exalts the standing of believers, it also gives them a calling to a higher pursuit by the direction and enabling power of the Lord. We are what we are by the grace of God so that we may serve for the glory of God. Specifically, Peter informs us that believers are privileged proclaimers of the excellent glories of the God who has wrought such amazing changes in their lives. This is not to say that all believers are called to be preachers of the gospel, but it is to say that all believers are to publish abroad, by their godly living, the glories of their saving God. Jesus puts this in terms of letting our lights shine in such a way that men might see our good deeds and glorify the Lord, who is the source of them (*Matt.* 5:16).

Our proclamation is not to be a self-regarding boasting, nor an ingratiating flattery, nor a focusing upon the trivial vanities that occupy the thoughts and energies of the unregenerate. We are rather to proclaim the excellencies of the saving God. With amazement and loving gratitude to the Lord for calling us from darkness and death to light and eternal life, we should by our words and deeds testify to others of the mercy and might of God in delivering sinners from guilt, bondage, corruption, and misery. We who have tasted and seen that the Lord is good should communicate that divine goodness to others. And this should be done naturally and not in any artificial way.

Nor should our proclamation be limited to testifying to men about our blessed Redeemer. We should proclaim to God and to his holy angels the excellencies of the Lord in our praises at times of worship. We should proclaim to the demons the glorious excellencies of our God by resisting their enticements and intimidations, honouring God by standing firm in his strength even in the evil day (*Eph.* 6:10–18).

THE GREAT CHANGE

The elect people of God are themselves wonders and have experienced many wonderful things. Peter lists several of those wonderful things in verse 9, and he sums them up in verse 10. In short, the apostle reminds us of what it is we have been made, and what we have received in Christ.

1. *Made a people.* Sin destroys all things. It not only alienates men from God, it also alienates people from each other. The scattered aliens to whom Peter wrote were conscious of their civil disenfranchisement and social banishment because of their faith. The more tragic reality of which Peter reminds them is that sin had dissolved their cohesion as a people, and that whatever bonds that seem to exist between sinners are illusionary. That has all changed for those in Christ. They have been forged into a people of like nature, status, and calling - the people of the living God, whose dominion is unlimited, whose love is immeasurable and unchanging, and whose power is almighty.

2. *Recipients of mercy.* It is understandable that scattered aliens should feel their deprivations keenly. Peter offers the compensation of the precious truth that, because of their faith, they had received

infinitely more than they had lost. What believers have in Christ is the saving mercy of God. That is the one thing necessary, the good and precious portion that will never be taken from them. Divine mercy is what sinners need most. Those who have it, have everything (*Rom.* 8:32). Those who lack it, have nothing of lasting value though they may possess the whole world (*Mark* 8:36).

Thus Peter shows in these verses something of the wonder and wealth of our salvation. From these truths we should learn to account all that we have in Christ as precious gain, and all that we have lost because of Christ as rubbish (*Phil.* 3:7–14).

The Practice of Purity

Beloved, I urge you as aliens and strangers to abstain from fleshly lusts, which wage war against the soul. [12] Keep your behavior excellent among the Gentiles, so that in the thing in which they slander you as evil doers, they may on account of your good deeds, as they observe them, glorify God in the day of visitation (1 Pet. 2: 11–12).

Peter has, in verses 4 to 10, described something of the rich and varied realities of the character and calling of the chosen people of God. The apostle has set out these truths in indicative statements. Now he follows these indicative roots with imperative fruits. Starting with verse 11 and continuing to 3:12, Peter appeals to his readers to apply the rich truths he has shared with them, personally to themselves. Those truths empower those feeding upon them by faith to live and serve in accordance with their position in Christ.

PERSONAL PURITY

Peter exhorts his readers in these verses to practise personal purity. His exhortation consists of a strong urging for believers to abstain from sinful lusts. By this urging, he alerts us to the fact that this is not an issue of minor importance. He reminds us that our Lord, who not only judges outward actions but also the heart, is far more concerned that his people avoid sin than that they avoid suffering. The carnal response to suffering is to become determined to find one's own pleasure at any cost - a supposedly deserved relief from the suffering. But the spiritual man will determine to resist sinful attitudes and actions. This exhortation of Peter's, and the determination it evokes in his readers to maintain moral purity, is far removed however from any censorious demand that suffering saints should fulfil an unpleasant but necessary duty.

1. *The call of love.* For the first time in this letter, Peter addresses his readers by the affectionate term, *beloved.* In 1:14, he referred to them familially as *children*, exhorting them to refuse to be conformed to their former lusts because they were called and destined to be holy like their heavenly Father. Love is implied by the use of the words, *children* and *Father.* But now Peter expressly uses a term that conveys to his readers that they are the objects of love, and that in two senses. Firstly, they are lovingly regarded by Peter himself. Though he is an apostle of Jesus Christ (1:1), with authority to rule over them, he knows that it is complementary, not contrary, to his apostolic authority to view and deal with his readers as beloved brethren.

The higher sense in which they are loved, however, is far more significant. They are beloved of God. The love of the Lord prompted him to accomplish the redemption of his people. It also prompts him to perfect the application of that redemption, not by indulging his people in their sinful lusts, but by lovingly calling them out of those lusts.

This love sets the true ground and context for this and all other exhortations, challenges, and commands in the Word of God. Because God has set his love upon us, we are precious in his sight. Because he predestined us in love to be his adopted sons (*Eph.* 1:4, 5) and is committed to conforming us to his holy image, we should view the calls in his Word for the maintenance of personal purity not as unwanted, unnatural intrusions into our private pleasures, but as his loving stimulation of us to the perfection of his holiness. And because God has so loved us we ought to view these exhortations as an opportunity for us to please our loving Lord, preserving ourselves for him, and refusing to defile ourselves and thus deprive him of the loving pleasure he takes in us.

2. *Believers' true alienation.* Fleshly lusts can seem so appealing and natural to believers at times, especially when the pain of suffering makes the saints long for some form of relief and pleasure. But the

giving in to fleshly lusts is neither appealing nor natural for those who are new creatures in Christ. In 1:1, Peter addressed his readers as scattered aliens. With the term, *aliens*, he was referring mainly to their civil, and perhaps geographic, alienation. Many of them were converted Jews who, through the Diaspora, were scattered from their national homeland. All of them, because of their faith in Jesus, were enduring increasing deprivation of their civil rights and protection.

Such geographic and civil alienation was however only the consequence of a far deeper alienation. The living God had called them out of the fallen, sinful, mass of humanity who were dead in sin and trespasses. The Lord had made them alive by regeneration, had justified them through faith, and had adopted them as citizens of his kingdom and heirs of his glory. That was a far more fundamental and blessed alienation for them. They had, by God's mercy, been alienated from all that was killing them, corrupting them, filling them with guilt and misery, and making them subject to God's righteous wrath.

This world, with its sinful pleasures and practices, is no longer the home and commonwealth of believers. Our citizenship is in heaven (*Eph.* 2:19–22). Through Christ, we are not only alienated from the world, but the world is also alienated from us (*Gal.* 6:14). We can take no relief or pleasure from the lusts of the flesh. The new nature we have in Christ, as well as the calling and enabling of God, concertedly orients us away from fleshly lusts and raises us to a faithful and loving contemplation of our heavenly home, and of that true and lasting happiness which only God can give.

3. *Abstinence from lusts.* Believers, who have by their salvation been made aliens from the guilt, corruption, and misery of this sinful world, should also alienate themselves from the residue of sinful lusts remaining in them. What does Peter mean when he uses the term, *lusts*? We may define these lusts as overmastering desires, as strong compulsions to possess and enjoy, they are particularly the desires for sexual gratification and the appetites for unrestricted sensual gratification. In short, lusts are pleasures that become ends in themselves. By his lust, a man attempts to sever God, the Giver of all things, from those legitimate gifts he would confer according to his wise, holy, and loving aims. With lust, we become determined to

override God's giving and take the pleasures for ourselves. But this is the suicide of all true, deeply satisfying and lasting pleasure. For it is God alone who, at his right hand, has pleasures for us forevermore (*Psa.* 16:11).

Peter, therefore, prescribes to us the only effective way that we can deal with such lusts, namely, that we abstain from them. As Joseph fled from the lustful enticements of Potiphar's unfaithful wife (*Gen.* 39:12), we must run from our lusts. By stout refusal to indulge them, we must starve them out of our lives. For no one can handle them or tame them, and the longer we consider them, the more compellingly attractive they become to us.

4. *Enticements are enemies.* Fleshly lusts appeal to us with potent promises of pleasure. They entice us with purported relief from pain and with thrilling prospects of satisfaction. But Peter makes clear that they are not the beautiful and pleasurable friends they would have us believe them to be. They are enemy soldiers, disguised under cloaks of proffered pleasure, but equipped to deliver only the deepest, sorest, most destructive pain. Our lusts wage war not simply against our reputations and relationships with others. They wage war against our souls. Our partaking of them involves a hidden cost which is unbearable. Peter has faithfully exposed that hidden cost to us, so that we might keep our affections fixed only on Christ, the true Lover of our souls, and make no provision for the flesh (*Rom.* 13:13,14).

PUBLIC PRACTICE

From his urging believers to maintain personal purity, Peter proceeds to direct them with respect to correct public practice. As a man thinks in his heart, so is he (*Prov.* 23:7). Private purity will shine out of the hearts of the Lord's beloved people in their public behaviour. The high standard of their behaviour will also have its effect upon the public sphere in which it is demonstrated.

1. *God's excellence, not man's expectations.* Men of the world expect low and vile things from those around them. By their own lusts they judge others to be as they themselves are. When a person rises above the low expectations of the world, it surprises the worldly, as Peter

writes later (4:4). It is to the high standard of God that Peter here calls his readers.

The pure hearts and minds of believers are not merely to be emptied of lusts but, instead, are to be filled with godly thoughts and affections. We are to be heavenly minded (*Col.* 3:1–4). We are to meditate upon the things of the Lord, all of which are honourable, right, pure, lovely, and excellent (*Phil.* 4:8).

But this godly attitude must also be exercised in action (*Phil.* 4:9). So Peter calls on believers not simply to refrain from sinful behaviour, but positively to do such deeds of godly and loving excellence that those around them who dwell in moral darkness will see their lights shining, and will, at the very least, be compelled to be ashamed of their ridicule and slander of believers (*Matt.* 5:16).

2. *Results of excellent living.* A life lived by the grace and for the glory of God is a high and blessed end in itself. Every victory we achieve over lustful temptation, every deed of loving-kindness we do for another in the name of Christ is, in a sense, its own reward. Yet, Peter informs us, such living can and does serve for the good of others, dead in their sins. Our excellent living not only serves to vindicate us from men's slander, it also may serve to convert sinful slanderers into brethren, who will then no longer curse us, but rather bless us and glorify our God.

The turning of worldly men to God on account of our godly living may not happen quickly, but it will surely occur. By the final day of God's visitation in judgment, we shall see that some surprising conversions will have taken place, having been, to some extent, prompted by our piety. There can be no higher and more satisfying incentive to motivate us to obey these exhortations delivered by Peter.

12

Civil and Social Graces

Submit yourselves for the Lord's sake to every human institution,
whether to a king as the one in authority, [14] or to governors as
sent by him for the punishment of evil doers and the praise of
those who do right. [15] For such is the will of God that by doing
right you may silence the ignorance of foolish men. [16] Act as free
men, and do not use your freedom as a covering for evil, but use
it as bondslaves of God. [17] Honor all men; love the brotherhood,
fear God, honor the king (1 Pet. 2:13–17).

In these verses, Peter further specifies the public outworking of that personal purity he had urged upon his readers in verses 11 and 12. The apostle gives instruction regarding Christian behaviour in two areas: civil and social. We learn from what Peter says that personal morality forms the basis for true and right civic and social responsibility. Those who maintain personal purity by the grace and enabling power of the Lord, are directed and empowered by the Lord to be the best and most practical citizens and neighbours to their fellow-men.

CIVIC RESPONSIBILITY

As Christians, we are to be in the world though not of the world. Our Lord Jesus, in his high priestly prayer, specifically asked his Father not to take believers out of the world, but to keep them from evil (*John* 17:15). By our regeneration, we are raised out of the world of death, sin, and godlessness, and in that sense, we are no longer of the world (*John* 17:16; *Col.* 3:3). Yet, we live out this new life in the midst of the old world of godless sinners. This creates a tension within us, so that God has to command us to abstain from fleshly lusts (verse 11). The psalmist tells us that the blessed man refrains from walking in the counsel of the wicked (*Psa.* 1:1). Yet, we are not to do this by any disengagement of ourselves from the world of sinful men.

It might be less difficult for us to maintain personal purity if we withdrew from the world and lived like hermits. It would be easy for us to defy and despise civil authorities that are not Christian. However, Peter makes clear that the believer's calling is to work out his faith through a right submission to the civil governments that God has ordained, and over which he sovereignly rules in this world.

1. *Submission to civil authority.* When Peter calls his readers to submit to the institutions of human society, he adds a qualification that alerts us to the fact that he is defining and limiting the extent of that submission. This qualification is contained in the words, *for the Lord's sake.* This means that the call for submission is not a call to slavish subservience to a wicked tyranny. Our submission is limited by considerations of what is and what is not sin in the sight of our Lord. Thus, for example, when Daniel's friends, Shadrach, Meshach, and Abed-nego, were ordered by Nebuchadnezzar to worship a golden image, they rightly refused to submit since their obedience would have been a violation of the first commandment (*Dan.* 3). Likewise, Peter and John, when ordered by the Sanhedrin not to proclaim the name of Jesus, responded: *We must obey God, rather than men* (*Acts* 5:29).

However, in obeying God, we can and should go a long way toward obeying legitimately constituted civil authority. We are to draw the line of submission only when we are being ordered by such an authority to sin. Even then, we are called to be most respectful in our refusal to obey sinful orders and laws. The ground and warrant for the unceasing respect we are to have for civil magistrates is that all civil authority comes from God (*Rom.* 13:1–7).

2. *Civil authority defined.* Peter stipulates the legitimate governing officials of his day. He speaks of kings or civil executives, and of governors or civil administrators. By thus mentioning two echelons

of civil rulers, Peter is informing us that he is calling for our submission to a whole order of civil authority. Our focus is to be on that order and the offices within it, not upon the man occupying the office. God, who is a God of order and not confusion (*1 Cor.* 14:33), is the sovereign superintendent over all civil order. And because our God is a God of order, we are called to recognize that even bad government is better than no government. Accordingly, we should commit ourselves to being the best citizens possible. This call by Peter for Christians to submit to the king - indeed, to honour the king (verse 17) – is remarkable when we recall that the king, or emperor, when Peter wrote was the despotic Nero.

3. *Incentives for submission.* Peter does not call for his readers to submit to civil authority without also providing certain incentives to encourage their submission. On the lowest level, Peter declares that believers' submission to civil authorities tends to keep them from being punished as evil doers, and leads them to be praised as those who do right. While it is true that even the best governments are imperfect in their punishment of evil doers and their rewarding of the righteous, it is also true that even the most godless governments recognize, for pragmatic reasons if for no other, the reliable nature of righteous men and the subversive nature of evil men.

A higher incentive is the apologetic effect the civil submission of Christians will have on their rulers and neighbours. Peter mentions this in verse 15, where he draws a connection between believers doing right and the silencing of foolish men who ignorantly slander Christians as being evil doers (verse 12).

In the days when Peter wrote, people who did not understand the Christians' practice of the Lord's Supper accused them of cannibalism. Those who did not understand the loving bond of fellowship between brothers and sisters in Christ accused believers of being incestuous. Those who did not understand the allegiance of the redeemed to Jesus, their Lord of lords and King of kings, accused believers of being seditious. Nothing then served better, nor serves better today, to reduce, if not completely silence, such calumnies as the right acting and good citizenship of the saints. It demonstrates to the men of this cursed world that those whose citizenship is in heaven (*Phil.* 3:20) are blessings to any earthly nation in which they dwell. What civil magistrate would not prefer having people who exhibit the fruit of the Spirit (*Gal.* 5:22–23) as compared to those manifesting the deeds of the flesh (*Gal.* 5:19–21) as citizens of his realm?

The highest incentive of all that Peter gives for submitting to civil authorities is that by doing so we obey the will of God. Our sovereign, heavenly Father is the King above all kings. Rulers arise and reign by his wise and holy ordaining. Even wicked, pagan nations like Babylon and Rome served the sinless purposes of God. That is why Jeremiah, for example, told the Jews suffering under the Babylonian scourge, applied to them by God because of their sin, to serve the king of Babylon and live (*Jer.* 27:17). Our submission to governing authorities is part of our obedience to God, who institutes the powers that be for his glory and our good.

SOCIAL GRACES

The salvation we have from sin, and the citizenship we have in heaven, together set us free from the dominion of sin and the tyranny of the most godless rulers. The Son of God has set his people free, and they are free indeed (*John* 8:36).

1. *True freedom.* Our freedom in Christ is not a licence for us to act rebelliously or disrespectfully toward civil authorities. We are not to attempt to cover such evil actions with the false claim that the King of kings has released us from our obligation to submit to authority. It is that King of kings who gave the fifth commandment, where he explicitly directs us to honour our parents, and implicitly directs us to respect his authority as it is exercised sinlessly through the government of sinful men. We best exercise our freedom when we take our directions from our heavenly Master whose bondslaves, Peter reminds us, we are.

Christian freedom is the freedom to know and do the will of God. The divine will is not only that we obey civil magistrates, but also that we act with becoming consideration and manners toward all men in every social context. Such manners are the soothing balm of all social interaction. If we reflect upon this matter, we shall find that whereas we only occasionally have opportunity to demonstrate our submission to civil magistrates, we have almost unceasing occasion to be mannerly toward our neighbours.

2. *Right relations*. Peter does not elaborate on the right attitudes we should have toward those listed in verse 17. He simply mentions a word to the wise sons of the infinitely wise God.

He calls upon his readers to honour all men. By this he means that we are not only to respect governing authorities, but also to seek to find and affirm the best in all people. For the Christian, the way to advance in nearness to God is not by tearing down, but by building up his fellow-men.

When it comes to our brethren in Christ, believers are not only to honour them but also to cherish them. To so love each and every member of the household of faith is the new commandment given to us by Jesus (*John* 13:34), and affirmed by the apostles Paul (*Rom.* 13:8), John (*1 John* 3:11, 23), and Peter.

Of all the men whom Peter's readers are called upon to honour, the highest, civil executive is due the highest honour, whether he be emperor, king, president, or prime minister. His person may be despicable - as in the case of Nero, under whose rule many Christians, including eventually Peter himself, would be put to death - but his position is instituted by and reflective of the authority of God. Thus we are to honour and pray for those whom God has placed over us (*1 Tim.* 2:1-4).

Above all, believers are to fear the Lord. Such reverence for God is the sustaining source of all civic responsibility and social grace. When we rightly regard the Lord above all men, it is then that we rightly regard all men.

Peter thus calls believers into a giving and serving mode. They are to pay respect to all men and to pray for all men, especially those in highest office, however godless their persons and policies may be. This may seem a hard call for the scattered believers to whom Peter was writing, suffering as they were under Nero's administrators and subjects. Yet those who are in Christ can afford to be paying their respects to, and offering their prayers for, such men because the people of God have been enriched and empowered for this calling by the King who is above all kings.

13

Working Relationships

Servants, be submissive to your masters with all respect, not only to those who are good and gentle, but also to those who are unreasonable. ¹⁹ For this finds favor, if for the sake of conscience toward God a man bears up under sorrows when suffering unjustly. ²⁰ For what credit is there if, when you sin and are harshly treated, you endure it with patience? But if when you do what is right and suffer for it you patiently endure it, this finds favor with God (1 Pet. 2: 18–20).

The salvation of which Peter writes is to be worked out in every area and circumstance of life. The grace of God operating in the souls of men finds a right way to exert itself in whatever station a believing man may find himself. The gospel of Christ does not necessarily call men to aspire to higher social and economic positions, but rather changes their hearts so that they learn how to glorify God whatever their estate.

HARDEST CASES CONSIDERED

Peter, in these verses, gives instruction for the application of grace to the worst and hardest of work relationships. If the grace of God can enable a man in the extremely challenging position of slavery to live to the glory of God, such grace can enable any person in less trying positions to live and work so as to glorify his redeeming Lord.

It is slaves that are the ones addressed by the apostle in these verses. We may wonder why Peter does not instruct masters as well, thus helping to make the plight of the slave less severe. Paul did this very thing when he brought both slaves and masters under the rule of Christ (*Eph.* 6:5–9; *Col.* 3:22–4:1). However, there may have been few, if any, masters among the scattered aliens to whom Peter was writing. It is also clear that Peter intends to address those of higher standing implicitly, while addressing those of lowest standing explicitly. Slaves were most vulnerable to abuse, suffering, injury, and indignity. They were in a position that would make them the likeliest candidates for dejection, despair, or anger. Their lot was unenviable to all, including themselves, so that given any direction and empowering they would think only in terms of rebellion against their slavery. Peter, however, gives different directions as he points to enabling grace.

1. *The duty.* For the Christian, victim status is not an option. Men dead in their sins may claim that they are victims, and truly believe that they are. It escapes their notice that they have brought most of their miseries upon themselves. Furthermore, they, being dead in sin, have no effective armour to protect themselves against the sinful exploitation of others.

The Christian however is made alive in Christ and is provided with the full armour of God to protect himself against the assaults of wicked men and devils (*Eph.* 6:10–18). Therefore no writer of Scripture ever addresses his readers as powerless victims of circumstances. Rather, God speaks to us in his Word as those whom he has made more than conquerors in Christ (*Rom.* 8:31–39).

Peter has already enumerated many of the resources common to all believers. He has spoken in Chapter 1 of the blessings of salvation: the regenerating work of God; the great and precious promises of the Lord; the living hope of believers; and the sanctifying refinement which is at work in them. The imperatives now addressed to slaves are based upon those enabling blessings. Peter therefore emphasizes immediately the responsibility that slaves have before God.

He does not call or even encourage slaves to change their station in this life. The distinctions between men, which they judge to be so important, are only provisional and not nearly so absolute as men conceive them to be. The radical and absolute change comes to a man when he is regenerated by God, justified, and adopted into the family of the heavenly King of kings. That change confers on all believers every spiritual blessing in heaven (*Eph.* 1:3). Thus it is really almost an indifferent matter whether a man completes his pilgrimage through this world as a prince or as a pauper, as a master or a slave.

What Peter does stress is the responsibility that slaves have to be submissive to their masters. It is not man but God who calls them to fulfil this duty. The God who calls them to the duty also enables them by his grace to fulfil it. He has also provided them with the supreme and perfect example of One who has submitted to the role of a servant, namely his own incarnate Son (*Mark* 10:45).

By their submission, believing slaves are to have an attitude of respect for the position, if not for the person, of their masters. They are to render diligent service, and to do so even when no one but their heavenly Master sees and knows what they are doing and why (*Eph.* 6:5,6).

2. *The extent of duty.* There are limits to the responsibility of believing slaves to submit obediently to their masters. This line is not drawn, however, where man would draw it. Human resentment flares up when a person receives harsh treatment. That resentment makes a person feel justified in his rebellion against, or flight from, his abusing superior. Peter, however, calls upon all in subservient positions to endure with grace, not only gentle and kind treatment, but also harsh and unreasonable treatment from their superiors.

Where, then, is the line of limitation for the obedience of believing slaves? It is found expressed in verse 13, where we are all called upon to submit to every human institution for the Lord's sake. Implied in this is that a slave's duty to submit ends at the point where he is asked to commit sin. There is no sin involved when one suffers abuse. Jesus suffered abuse and by it he redeemed his people. We are all inclined to spare ourselves inconvenience, humiliation, and suffering because we fail to see and to believe that God has used and will use those grim tools for our good and his glory.

REASONABLE SERVICE

Peter does not call slaves to be submissive even to abusive masters on the basis of expediency. He is not urging passivity and compliance upon the slaves merely in order to keep them from angering, and being punished or killed by, their masters. Rather, the apostle bases his instruction upon right and reasonable spiritual principles.

1. *For conscience.* The call for believing slaves to be submissive to their masters is a call for them to maintain a clear conscience before God. The first sin committed in the world, and the root of all other sins, was man's rebellion against his heavenly Maker and Master. God gives his saving grace to believers, not so that they might rebel against those human institutions he has ordained, but rather in order that they might serve conscientiously within them, transforming them for the better.

The Holy Spirit of God opens the eyes of believers so that they may see and serve their redeeming God in all situations. The redeemed are taught to believe that God causes all things, even adverse things, to work together for their good (*Rom.* 8:28). It is to the holy, wise, and good purposes of the Lord in adverse situations that believers - whether slave or free - are submitting. Believers thus serve, prompted by a God-centred conscience, not by man's coercion. The Lord, who gives his people an enlightened and righteously sensitive conscience, rewards with greater grace those who obey its holy promptings.

2. *For credit.* The principled submission of slaves may or may not be noted and rewarded by their masters. But the heavenly Master of all believers sees and blesses his suffering yet humble and diligent servants (*Col.* 3:22–24). God regards most highly those whose submission to unjust abuse clearly reflects the redeeming sufferings of his beloved Son. The favouring grace God gives to his suffering servants is more than abundant reward for their faithful patience and trusting submissiveness. It sustains them in time and works for them in eternity a weight of glory beyond all comparison (*Rom.* 8:18; *2 Cor.* 4:16–18).

FOCUS OF FAITH

The duty of submissiveness to which Peter calls Christian slaves is one that can only be fulfilled by faith. The object of that faith can never be man. Therefore the gentleness or harshness of a slave's master is not really relevant. Men may threaten or reward, flatter or flatten as they will. The focus of a Christian slave's faith is to be on God, not men.

It is the heavenly Master of those who are in the most vulnerable and least enjoyable positions who will protect them and reward them in their service. The provision of God is most lavish and potent. The Lord can sustain his servants amidst most unjust and cruel circumstances. We need but think of Joseph (*Gen.* 37–50) and how God used all of his long and harsh servitude in order to prepare him for his exalted and saving service. The wise and righteous King of heaven can overrule earthly masters, sinlessly causing even their sinful exploitation of his people to serve for their promotion.

If our Lord has made such abundant provision of his enabling grace for believers who are suffering as slaves, how much more should we who are free from the bondage of men, and who endure little more than the annoyance of men, bear patiently and perseveringly the little adversities that we face? If the least and lowest class of men, redeemed by Christ, are secured and made certain of ultimate, glorious exaltation, surely those of us who, in God's providence, have obtained higher social and economic standing and means, have no less divine provision.

14

The Example of the Suffering Saviour

*For you have been called for this purpose, since Christ also
suffered for you, leaving you an example for you to follow in His
steps, ²² who committed no sin, nor was any deceit found in His
mouth; ²³ and while being reviled, He did not revile in return;
while suffering, He uttered no threats, but kept entrusting
Himself to Him who judges righteously; ²⁴ and He Himself bore
our sins in His body on the cross, that we might die to sin and
live to righteousness; for by His wounds you were healed. ²⁵ For
you were continually straying like sheep, but now you have
returned to the Shepherd and Guardian of your souls* (1 Pet.
2:21–25).

The focus of the Christian is ever to be *Christ*. Even when we
suffer harsh and unjust treatment, our vision should be set not
on our own afflictions, still less upon any contemplated measures of
revenge against our oppressors, but rather upon our saving God. As
an incentive for believers to submit to inescapable suffering, the
apostle has noted the favour that such submission finds with God
(verse 20). However, God does more than take pleasure in, and
provide grace for, those who are submissive to the sufferings he has
sovereignly ordained for them. At the heart of the gospel is the truth
that God, in the Person of his Son, has borne our sufferings for us,
not in order that we might escape all suffering, but so that we might
victoriously and sanctifyingly endure our afflictions.

Jesus has both endured the sufferings that our sins deserved, and
provided for us an encouraging example of godly submission to

suffering. Therefore, Peter instructs his readers as to the true nature of their sufferings. The pains endured even by the least privileged amongst them, such as the slaves, were not to be seen as some dreadful calamity but as a purposeful course set before them by the Lord.

THE CALL TO SUFFER

Suffering for the Christian is not a curse but a calling for them to walk in the way that their Master went as he accomplished their salvation. The fact that we are not helpless victims in our afflictions, and that our sufferings do not befall us by chance, should overcome our dread of suffering, and fill us with hope. If we are called to bear afflictions, we are to consider both our calling and the One who issues the call.

1. *Those called.* It is natural for all men to face suffering pragmatically. That is to say, people tend naturally to avoid pain and seek pleasure. No man would endure, still less welcome, afflictions unless he were convinced that they served a higher purpose for his good. It is precisely such a higher purpose that Peter brings into view when he writes that believers have been called patiently to endure harsh and unjust treatment.

Believers endure their pains not as victims but as those fulfilling a vocation. They are called to stand fast and, by appropriating the grace of the Lord, to bear their sufferings for the glory of God and for the higher good of their own souls. We who are in Christ should be conscious that in our furnaces of affliction, we are fulfilling purposes that are higher, wiser, and more loving than we can know.

Christ has not only expiated the sins of his people, he has, in doing so, set an example his people are called to follow. Paul speaks of his own sufferings as a filling up that which is lacking in Christ's sufferings (*Col.* 1:24). This does not mean that the atoning sufferings of our Redeemer were only partial and needing to be augmented by what we suffer. Rather, it speaks of a precious and intimate communion, or fellowship, of suffering (*Phil.* 3:10), between the Captain of salvation and the members of his Church Militant.

Peter tells us that Jesus in his sufferings left us an example to follow. The word translated, *example*, is a Greek word used only here in the New Testament. It means writing placed under tracing paper for the purpose of exact copying. We are called literally to trace the course, that is, to follow in the footsteps of Christ's sufferings, who endured supreme afflictions as he accomplished the highest good for others and manifested the clearest and most profound demonstration of God's glory.

2. *The One calling.* If believing slaves are called to bear patiently the abuses of their harsh masters, this clearly implies that someone issues the call. In this case, it is the Lord of glory, the divine King of kings, who calls his people to endure their afflictions secure in the knowledge that their circumstances result from his sovereign wisdom, immeasurable love, and almighty power.

Peter was no mere theorist when he wrote of the divine calling and purpose in the sufferings of the believing slaves. This very apostle, along with John, had suffered at the hands of the Sanhedrin after they had healed the lame beggar at the gate of the temple (*Acts* 3:1–10). The apostles were arrested and threatened not to speak or teach further in Jesus' name (*Acts* 4:17–21). Above the sinful abuses and threats of the members of the Sanhedrin, the apostles and their brethren rightly saw the superintending hand of God, to whom they cried, not for release from their sufferings, but for boldness and faithfulness to Jesus in those afflictions (*Acts* 4:24–30).

If we are called by God to endure harsh treatment, we need not fear that such treatment will ultimately ruin us. Rather, we should reckon that he who calls us will keep us in our afflictions, bringing forth great good for us from them.

THE SUPREME EXAMPLE OF SUFFERING

The endurance of momentary pain for higher gain is a dynamic with which all men are familiar. Analogies such as an athlete in training, or a patient undergoing life-saving surgery illustrate the benefit of submission to certain types of pain. However, it is hard, indeed impossible, for us to see the benefit to be derived from submission to the harsh and unjust abuses of wicked men.

The key to unlocking the treasures hidden in sanctifying suffering is found by contemplating the Saviour's sufferings on the cross. The seemingly meaningless maltreatment suffered by those members of the Kingdom of God least able to avoid it, such as these believing slaves, is seen to be highly significant when viewed in the light of the Saviour's supreme example of suffering.

Peter employs the relative pronoun, *who*, at the beginning of each verse in verses 22 to 24. He does this so as to fix the attention of his readers upon the One who suffered to accomplish their salvation. He touches briefly on several facets of the sufferings of Christ in order to provide true context and understanding for those who suffer because of their faithful following of Jesus.

1. *The Perfection of the Sufferer.* The sufferings of Jesus were not as a result of his sin. It should not surprise sinners therefore when they are harshly and unjustly treated. By our sin, we treat God with ingratitude and rebellion. The Puritans rightly referred to sin as an attempt to murder God. We may feel more keenly the pain of our afflictions when they are harshly and unjustly administered. However, we do well to recall that as sinners we never suffer in this life what we deserve. Jesus, on the other hand, did not deserve to suffer at all. He committed no injurious sin against God or man. But no one has ever suffered as deeply as he did.

Our Saviour, however, did not experience his afflictions as a hapless victim. He, rather, voluntarily submitted to them in pursuit of his calling to accomplish the redemption of God's people. This gracious, glorious, and purposeful result of his sufferings is implied by the Scripture to which Peter refers in verses 22 to 24. The apostle quotes from Isaiah 53, that classic Old Testament passage on the Suffering Servant. As his sufferings had an unspeakably glorious result, so we who follow in his steps, as we heed the divine calling, should expect our suffering to be productive of glory (*2 Cor.* 4:17).

Not only did Jesus commit no sin, there was not even guile in his speech. His actions, words, and intentions were always pure, true, and right. This reference to the Saviour's lack of guile is especially instructive for the slaves whom Peter was addressing. They were probably tempted to think that their only resource for easing, if not escaping, their harsh treatment would have been speech calculated to flatter or mislead their masters. As Jesus prevailed over his afflicting enemies not by trickery, but by truth, so too believers are called to persevere and to prevail by speaking the truth in love, even to those who would abuse them.

2. *The Patience of His Sufferings.* Jesus was not esteemed, but rather reviled by his enemies. Nor was his endurance of such abuse occasional, but it was a continual feature of his public ministry. His first sermon was met with rage and with an attempt to throw him over the cliff of Nazareth's city hill (*Luke* 4:16–30). His disciples often misunderstood his mission, while his own family at times thought him insane (*Mark* 3:21). He was reviled by Pharisees, Sadducees, and ordinary people, especially when on the cross (*Matt.* 27:42). The reviling that he received did not prompt him to retaliate; he endured his afflictions silently. The sufferings heaped upon him did not draw threats and curses from him, nor those responses which, given his harsh and unjust treatment, might seem natural and inevitable.

It was not fear or shock that compelled Jesus to suffer silently. His constant afflictions were borne with a secure serenity because he continually delivered himself trustingly into the caring hands and the righteous judgment of his heavenly Father. Men cried for his crucifixion, but Jesus put on the armour of the Father's approval. Men hated him, but God owned him as his beloved and well-pleasing Son. Those who are Christ's are similarly called to reckon by faith that though wicked men may afflict them, the God of heaven holds them as objects of his affection, and accepts them in his beloved Son (*Eph.* 1:6).

3. *The Depth and Design of His Sufferings.* Our Saviour did not suffer stoically. His passion was greater even than a noble endurance of afflictions. The depth and divine purpose of his sufferings are touched on in verse 24. He himself – that is to say, no one other than or less than the incarnate Son of God – bore our sins in that which he suffered. The word translated, *bore*, has the connotation of a priest carrying a sacrifice up to an altar. Peter had heard John the Baptist declare Jesus to be the Lamb of God who bears away the sin of the world (*John* 1:29), and he had read from Isaiah 53:4 of the Messiah

bearing our griefs. Thus it was that Jesus suffered for others, and his bearing of those sufferings had a redeeming result.

It was for our sins that Jesus suffered. Apart from any other logical necessity or philosophical understanding of why believers should suffer, it is more than enough that we know that he bore our sins. Out of an immeasurable sense of gratitude, we should be willing to follow his example of suffering.

Jesus bore our sins in his body. He not only endured the vicarious punishment for our sins, he became sin for us (*2 Cor.* 5:21). He bore wounds, or welts, in his body, just as the maltreated believing slaves here addressed had scars from their beatings, and he did so for the thorough healing and cleansing of those who had been mortally wounded and morally defiled by their sin. Indeed, he became a curse for sinners, as the reference to the cross (literally, *wood*) indicates. Slaves may be abusively cursed by their wicked masters, yet none of them ever were so deeply and thoroughly reckoned accursed as was Jesus. The Law of God makes clear that those who hang on a tree are not only guilty of crime, but accursed by God as sinners (*Deut.* 21:22, 23), a point made clear by Paul in Galatians 3:13.

The divine design of these exquisite sufferings of the Son of God is explained when Peter writes that it was in order that we might die to sin and live to righteousness. Literally, the words mean that we might continually be away from sin, while living to righteousness. Jesus suffered so that we might not sin, even when we are being subjected to severe suffering ourselves.

OUR SAFETY IN OUR SUFFERINGS

In verse 25, Peter progresses from the image of Christ having suffered as the sacrificial Lamb of God saving his people, to that of Christ serving as the Shepherd and overseer of his people. As the good Shepherd, Jesus has so committed himself to the protection of his sheep that he suffered and died so that they might live (*John* 10:11). This same Christ, who died for his people, is the resurrected One who ever lives to make intercession for them (*Heb.* 7:25). He oversees his people by his ever vigilant and loving care, providing for them by his holy wisdom, and protecting them by his almighty power.

We who are in Christ are safe, even when we suffer harsh and unjust treatment. We were not safe when we wandered sinfully from God. But now we have by God's gracious calling and enabling returned to our only wise, immeasurably loving, and omnipotently protecting Shepherd. If he makes us stay in afflictive circumstances, we shall in those circumstances find green pastures of his provision (*Psa*. 23:2). We shall not be destroyed if we follow his example of suffering. The glorious results of his sufferings – all ordained by God for our good – shed an empowering light on our afflictions, leading us to expect glorious and incomparably satisfying results from them (*2 Cor*. 4:16-18).

15

The Fruit of Faith in the Family

In the same way, you wives, be submissive to your own husbands so that even if any of them are disobedient to the word, they may be won without a word by the behavior of their wives, [2] as they observe your chaste and respectful behavior. [3] And let not your adornment be merely external – braiding the hair, and wearing gold jewelry, or putting on dresses; [4] but let it be the hidden person of the heart, with the imperishable quality of a gentle and quiet spirit, which is precious in the sight of God. [5] For in this way in former times the holy women also, who hoped in God, used to adorn themselves, being submissive to their own husbands. [6] Thus Sarah obeyed Abraham, calling him lord, and you have become her children if you do what is right without being frightened by any fear. [7] You husbands likewise, live with your wives in an understanding way, as with a weaker vessel, since she is a woman; and grant her honor as a fellow heir of the grace of life, so that your prayers may not be hindered (1 Pet. 3:1–7).

Faith fixed on Christ has impact not only upon the vertical relationship between God and man, but also upon the horizontal relationships between men. The heavenly doctrine regarding Christ and our salvation in him proves therefore to be of greatest earthly good as its application sweetens and sanctifies all human relationships. This is particularly true of that special and most intimate of human relationships, namely, the union of a man and woman in holy matrimony. Accordingly, Peter proceeds to give instruction regarding the behaviour expected of husbands and wives in Christian marriage.

PRELIMINARY CONSIDERATIONS

Before we proceed to examine the explicit teaching of this passage, we do well to ponder some preliminary considerations. Several questions should arise in our minds from a realization of what Peter does, and what he does not, write, and of whom he does, and whom he does not, address in these verses.

1. *Why such emphasis on wives?* Peter devotes six verses of instruction to wives, and only one to husbands. Perhaps there were more women in the churches to which the apostle wrote. From verse 1 we may gather that a number of believing wives had unbelieving husbands. In addition, wives face particular temptations when they and their families are suffering, as the original readers of the letter were.

Under pressure of persecution, wives may fear that their husbands will fail to protect and provide for their families. Such fearful wives can find themselves tempted to assume leadership of the family. Therefore Peter devotes attention to these and similar temptations that wives may face, and which may not prove such strong temptations to their husbands.

2. *Where are the children?* Peter instructs husbands and wives, but says nothing to the children of these covenant families. It may be that Peter expects his readers to remember Paul's fuller teaching about the family, which includes references to children, as found in Ephesians 5:22–6:4 and Colossians 3:18–21. In Peter's second epistle – which may or may not have been addressed to the same readers – the apostle explicitly refers his readers to Paul's writings (*2 Pet.* 3:15–16). More probably, however, Peter rightly reckons that as the parents fare, so also will their children fare. Godly and loving husbands and wives best portray and convey to their children the salvation of Christ. Peter therefore concentrates upon the parents in this passage.

3. *Why press duties upon a delightful relationship?* Marriage is a relationship based upon mutual love shared by the partners. The duties pressed by Peter upon Christian husbands and wives may seem contrary to the delight of love. Yet, even redeemed sinners in process of sanctification require the regulating of their lives by the holy and loving wisdom of the Lord. We do not know how to love as we ought, but God, who is love, directs us by his Word, and empowers us by his Spirit rightly to love one another.

4. *What is here for the unmarried?* Not all who originally received this letter or have read it through the ages, have been married. Is there a word in this passage for those who are single? Through this teaching, those who are single gain understanding as to how they should pray for their married brethren, and for themselves in preparation for their own possible marriage. Also, since the grace of God in Christ is fundamental in this most intimate of human relationships, an increased understanding of Christian marriage teaches us more about the love our heavenly Bridegroom has for us, and the response we should make to that love.

WORDS FOR WIVES

From what Peter has written at the end of the second chapter concerning the submission of Christ to the will of his Father and the work of our redemption, the apostle draws out an application for believing wives. They are directed to be submissive to their husbands. The context of this call for submission is clearly therefore an emphasis that Christian submission is not degrading and grovelling, but is rather a voluntary fruit of holy love.

1. *Submission to your husband.* Believing wives are directed to be *submissive.* This direction is not a call for women to be generally submissive to all men, though a deferring respect for all others ought to characterize the attitude of all believers (*Phil.* 2:3–4). Rather, wives are told to be submissive to their own husbands. A Christian wife is called to be a supportive helpmeet, not to a stranger or tyrant, but to the one man on earth given to her by God in the bonds of holy, matrimonial love. A wife's help

ceases when she endeavours to become the leading head of her marriage.

The nature and extent of this submission can be determined by what Peter writes in the following verses (as well as by what Paul has written elsewhere in Scripture). For example, wives are to be submissive *in the Lord* (*Eph.* 5:22; *Col.* 3:18). This means that a wife's submission to her earthly husband should be a fruit of her submission to Christ. It further means that she does not submit to sin, for that would be rebellion against her heavenly Head. However, Peter's directive for the submission of wives to their husbands indicates that believing wives can go further than any would naturally be inclined to go in their submissive support of their husbands, without crossing the line of sin. It is the crossing of that line, and not the crossing of their own wills, that determines the rightful extent of their submission.

2. *Worst case scenario.* The believing wife's submissiveness to her husband is not dependent upon the husband's obedience to the Lord. A man may be an unbeliever or a disobedient believer, and still, in everything short of sin, a Christian wife owes him submissive obedience. This obligation should not be viewed as a painful burden. Rather, Peter makes clear that in Christ there is gracious divine provision for the worst case. There is a Christ-honouring way for a weaker vessel to live in even the worst marriage. Peter goes on to say how such grace is appropriated.

3. *Words and actions.* A wife's submissive attitude does more than anything else could to sweeten even a bitter marriage and to soften a hard-hearted husband. Yet, frequently, when a Christian wife's husband is disobedient to the teaching of God's Word, that wife feels tempted to show contempt for her husband, rather than submission. She may urge, threaten, and cajole him to see and do his godly duty. Even if she tries with gentle patience to bring his conscience under the Word, her efforts in that way are not sanctioned by Scripture. God clearly forbids women preachers in the Church (*1 Tim.* 2:12), and Peter makes clear that women preachers are not allowed in the home. Gracious, lovingly submissive conversation is allowed, but rarely, if ever, does a

husband in disobedience to God hear and heed the godly verbal appeals of his wife.

It is said rightly that the time for speaking comes rarely while the time for doing never departs. Peter makes clear to believing wives that the way to win their disobedient husbands is through their godly deeds, not through their proclamation of doctrine. When a wife behaves with moral purity, and with respect toward her husband because of her reverence for God, even unbelieving husbands cannot help but see such good works and find themselves inclined to glorify the God who is their source.

4. *Adornment and essence*. Peter adds an enhancing instruction to his counsel for wives to win their disobedient husbands without argument but with action. The actions of Christian wives must be sincere. The adornment of their lives by respectful deeds must not be a charade. Nor should they seek to pacify their unruly husbands, or find a sense of self-worth through a preoccupation with their physical beauty. Rather, in this case, as in all cases for a Christian, what she thinks in her heart is what she really is (*Prov.* 23:7).

It is the cultivation of her new essential nature before God and by God's gracious provision that should be the believing wife's aim. She sincerely submits to her husband for God's sake. With gentleness and humility she seeks lovingly to win her husband to Christ by portraying before him the essence of the Saviour – the One who calls all who labour and are heavy laden to himself, that they might find rest (*Matt.* 11:28, 29). Whether or not the husband of a godly wife responds favourably to her respectful manifestation of a quiet spirit, the King of glory finds her attitude and actions precious in his sight.

5. *Holy example*. Peter concludes his instructions to wives by setting before them the holy examples of Old Testament women. The chaste and gracious Abigail could live with a foolish husband like Nabal precisely because she set her sights and hopes upon God, not upon her husband (*1 Sam.* 25). Peter specifically mentions Sarah, whose characteristically submissive attitude toward her husband, Abraham, was manifested in the way she addressed him as lord (*Gen.* 18:12), and submitted to him as such. When Sarah was submissive

to Abraham, things went well; when she preached to the patriarch, Ishmael resulted. As Abraham is termed by Scripture the father of the faithful, so Peter raises up Sarah as a mother of all faithful Christian wives.

The humbling of themselves under God and the submitting of themselves to their husbands to which Peter calls Christian wives is no degradation. Instead, it lifts them to the position of daughters of holy Sarah, and makes them precious in the sight of God. Peter's final exhortation to such wives is that they resist fearing the ridicule of godless women and the resentment of their own disobedient husbands. These wives are called to have highest regard for their heavenly Husband, whose face they will one day behold as they reign with him forever (*Rev.* 22:4,5).

A WORD FOR HUSBANDS

Peter has fewer words to address to believing husbands, but they are no less challenging and encouraging than the many words written to their wives. It should be understood that much of what Peter wrote about wives appropriating God's grace to live graciously even with their disobedient husbands has application to husbands who find themselves living with disobedient wives. If God gives grace for the weaker vessel to be more than conqueror over her husband's disobedience, even more should a husband expect grace that he might live lovingly with a wife who is in rebellion from God and even from himself.

1. *Living with wives.* Christian husbands are exhorted by Peter to *live with their wives.* They are not to live for their careers or with their buddies, but are to live for and with their wives. Too many men in our day live out of their homes and away from their wives, and the lack of depth in their marriage reveals this.

Even more than merely living in physical proximity with their wives, believing men are to cultivate a sensitivity toward and a spiritual and emotional affinity with their wives. A husband is to know and understand his helpmeet. He is not to assume that she thinks and feels as he does, but is to exert himself in learning to fathom her thoughts and desires, her fears and delights.

A key to such understanding sensitivity is the man's realization that his wife is what Peter calls a *weaker vessel*. The so-called politically-correct people of our day maintain that women are as physically strong and emotionally tough as men. Many women in our day try to appear as strong and as tough as men, and they succeed not in becoming men, but only in becoming women of rough actions. Men know that women have vulnerabilities that they do not have. Unbelieving men exploit those vulnerabilities, reducing women to objects to gratify their base desires. Peter calls on men to recognize the vulnerability of their wives and act in protective and providing ways toward them, thus truly strengthening them in the love of the Lord.

2. *Honour and heirs*. Christian husbands are further exhorted to treat their wives with *honour*. As wives are to be respectfully submissive to their husbands, regardless of how deserving their husbands may be, so husbands are to grant honour to their wives not because of their deserving achievements, but because it is their due in Christ.

God originally created man and woman with a basic equality. The fact that Eve was made from Adam's rib – and not a bone from his head to show superiority, nor a bone from his foot to show inferiority – indicates basic equality of being. Adam, of course, preceded Eve in creation and was the federal head of the race, but it was sin that exaggerated the difference between men and women, relegating women to being subject to their husbands' dominion (*Gen.* 3:16). In Christ, the essential equality of men and women is restored, as Peter intimates when he refers to the wives as fellow-heirs of the grace of life with their husbands. The grace of new life in Christ ushers husbands and wives into a new order in which, when grace matures into glory, there will be neither male nor female (*Gal.* 3:28). There will still be order and differences, but the differences will be perfected into a glorious harmony of eternal life.

3. *Unhindered prayers*. Peter concludes this passage by giving to Christian husbands a sobering warning if they fail to cherish and honour their wives properly. Should a man fail to love his wife respectfully, he will find that God refuses to hear and heed his

prayers. The God who will not receive a man's worship if that man has something against his brother, or his brother has something against him (*Matt.* 5:23), will not receive a man's prayers if he has allowed anything but holy love to be manifested towards his wife and sister in Christ.

MUTUAL SUBMISSION IN CHRIST

The first verse of chapter three begins with the connecting phrase: *In the same way*. Similarly, verse 7 uses the connecting word: *likewise*. These words connect the exhortation that Peter gives to husbands and wives with that which he had previously written concerning Christ's loving service in which he voluntarily submitted himself to his Father's will.

The basis for the harmonious love in a Christian family is the loving harmony of the Triune God. Specifically, Christ's submission to his Father's will is the example for wives in their submission to their husbands, and Christ's saving and honouring love for his people is the example for husbands in their love for their wives. For those in the bonds of holy matrimony, their faithful submission to Christ will beget mutually faithful subjection to each other in love (*Eph.* 5:21-23).

16

A Summary of the Submissive Spirit

To sum up, let all be harmonious, sympathetic, brotherly, kindhearted, and humble in spirit; [9] not returning evil for evil, or insult for insult, but giving a blessing instead; for you were called for the very purpose that you might inherit a blessing. [10] For, 'Let him who means to love life and see good days refrain his tongue from evil and his lips from speaking guile. And let him turn away from evil and do good; let him seek peace and pursue it. For the eyes of the Lord are upon the righteous, and His ears attend to their prayer, but the face of the Lord is against those who do evil' (1 Pet. 3:8–12).

Peter has been expounding the discipline of Christian submission in the passage beginning at 2:13 and ending at 3:7. He has called for his readers to practise such submission in the civil realm (2:13–17), in the work place (2:18–25), and in their families (3:1–7). In these verses, the apostle sums up the spirit and godly fruits of such submission when exercised by believers in all areas of their lives.

A SUMMATION OF DIRECTIVES

Peter adds a final word which has reference to all that he has thus far written about Christian submission. When he writes, *let all be* . . . , we are to understand that the attitudes and actions he goes on to detail should characterize the determined practice of all believers in every situation and relationship of their lives. He lists the components of these attitudes in verse 8, and of righteous actions in verse 9.

A Summary of the Submissive Spirit

1. *Harmony*. The aim of the Christian is not to be to dominate others. Neither is his aim to be in cowering subjugation under others. Rather, believers are called by God to cultivate and exercise their gifts and graces, so far as it depends upon them, in an orderly, pleasing, and fruitful blending with the differing aspirations and actions of others.

Paul gives a beautiful picture of harmony in the assembly of God's people when he exhorts believers to speak the truth in love, thus enabling the whole body to grow in Christ by that which every joint supplies (*Eph.* 4:15–16). When diverse characters co-operate in loving righteousness, the result is neither a dull monotony nor a disintegrating chaos, but a melodic blending of diversity into a higher and more richly complex unity.

2. *Sympathy*. The holy harmony that should characterize the community of believers is not to be the result of staged actions or mechanical responses. We are not lifeless instruments producing a harmonious sound, but living souls endeavouring lovingly to cooperate with others. Our concern is not simply that we play our part, but also that we exercise an ever increasing sincere fellow-feeling for those with whom we cooperate. This sympathetic tenderness should prompt us to rejoice with those who rejoice and weep with those who weep (*Rom.* 12:15).

3. *Fraternity*. The exhortation for believers to manifest a *brotherly* quality is a call for those in Christ to recognize and, with loving respect, to cherish and cultivate their relational bonds in Christ. Men are tempted and inclined to disregard brotherly ties. The first man born into the world, Cain, did not cherish his brother, Abel, but murdered him (*Gen.* 4:1–8). Likewise, the ten oldest sons of Jacob sought to murder their brother, Joseph, before they resolved to sell him into slavery (*Gen.* 37:18–27). Malicious thoughts about, and vicious actions towards, others in the body of Christ can only take hold of us when we allow ourselves to forget the vital knowledge that those others are our brethren in the Lord. How much easier it is to honour and cherish other believers when we bear in mind that they, like ourselves, have been bought by the blood of the Saviour, and are children of our heavenly Father.

4. *Kindness*. We are to be *kind-hearted* toward others. This means that our hearts should manifest a charitable acceptance and toleration of others. Kindness is the tender and positive regard we have towards our kin. We love them and seek to exercise the judgment of charity toward them in spite of their failings. Kindness, which is part of the fruit of the Spirit (*Gal.* 5:22), breeds within us patience, which we lovingly exercise, especially when others manifest their faults or grow in grace more slowly than we think they should be doing. The kind person ever seeks to help, never to harm, others.

5. *Humility*. Peter instructs his readers to be *humble in spirit*. This means that we are not merely to affect humility, acting as if we were meek and mild servants of others, when our inner attitude is full of high ambition. Those who are humble in spirit are neither high-minded, nor easily offended, nor self-centred. Instead, the humble in spirit are oriented towards a loving service to others (*Phil.* 2:1–11).

All of the above attitudes had been learned by Peter himself. Admittedly, he had to learn them the hard way. But his proud and boasting ways had been replaced by humility and sympathetic brotherly kindness that enabled him to work in harmony with his fellow disciples. We find Peter being jealous of John in the Gospels, for example (*John* 21:21–22), but co-operating lovingly with John in the Book of Acts (*Acts* 3).

6. *Righteous responses*. In verse 9, Peter proceeds to mention the actions that should flow from the virtuous attitudes he listed in verse 8. Just as the five qualities listed in verse 8 are not exhaustive, but representative of a host of godly attitudes, so also the actions of verse 9 are the summaries of tendencies that should ever characterize the behaviour of believers. It should further be noted that the actions fall into a specific class of behaviour. Peter is writing particularly about the responses of believers to the unloving and unrighteous actions of others against them. The response of Christians to the evil they suffer should be guided by the standard of the Lord's righteousness, and not by their own sinful reasoning.

Our reaction to the evil deeds that others commit against us should be non-retaliatory. It may seem right to us that we repay others in the same coin as that which we received from them, but that is not right in the sight of God. We are not to fight the fire of evil with the fire of evil, thus corrupting ourselves by our wicked response. We are to control even our speech, not returning abusive words to those who have insulted us. Words are powerful tools for good or evil, and our Lord commands us to control our tongues, using them to express truth lovingly, and not to pour out the pollutions of sinful anger (*Eph.* 4:15; *James* 3:1–12).

Not only are believers exhorted not to resist evil with evil, they are even instructed to return good for evil. Our words and actions should convey blessing to others, even, and especially, to those least deserving such blessing. In this we are called to be like our Saviour, who bore supreme suffering and returned supreme blessing (*1 Pet.* 2:23–24).

By blessing rather than insulting those who commit evil against us, we allow the light of God's saving grace to shine from us so that others might be led to glorify God, the source of such gracious blessing (*Matt.* 5:10,11,16). Even if men are not converted by such blessing, their rejection of our gracious response will but call forth burning coals of divine wrath against them (*Rom.* 12:19–21). This wrath of the Lord is untainted by sin and descends with unadulterated righteousness upon its deserving objects in a way that our polluted and egotistic sinful retaliation could never do.

SOURCE AND GOAL OF DIRECTIVES

Peter, having set out directives for believers' attitudes and actions, proceeds to speak of the ground and goal of such directives. The ground is our calling by God, and the goal is our blessing. We are taught this in the Holy Scriptures so that we might be certain how we are to think and act in relation to others.

1. *Our calling*. Peter informs us that believers are called to live in the harmonious and gracious way represented in verses 8 and 9. We have been called by God, not only to follow the example of Christ's suffering (2:21), but also to manifest our Saviour's sympathetic humility in all circumstances. We are called to know Christ, to be like Christ, and to act like Christ in all things.

2. *Our blessing.* The call for us to be and act in this Christ-like way is a call for us to give *blessing* to others. It may seem costly and sacrificial to us when we with humility and sympathetic love bless even those who curse us. But the giving of such blessing returns to us. What Jesus said about it being more blessed to give than to receive is especially true when we give such blessing to those who have been evil towards us. To do so may serve to melt the hearts of those heaping evil and insult upon us. They may be convicted and brought to conversion by the return of blessing for their cursing. If so, they will cease their cursing, and will heap gratitude upon us. However, even if the recipients of our blessings do not return them, God is committed to blessing his children who obey him in blessing others.

3. *Precept and promise of Scripture.* Peter supports the exhortation given in verses 8 and 9 by quoting several verses from Psalm 34. The first part of the passage he quotes is negative. We are neither to utter evil speech nor to employ deceptive communications. Our cursing and misleading of our enemies may seem to be the way that security and satisfaction can be attained. But the one who wants to have a long and good life resists returning evil for evil. We are also to take no evil action against others. To use evil in response to evil will only corrupt, weaken, and injure us, and will fail utterly to subdue or vanquish our persecutors.

The second half of the passage quoted sets out positive duty. We are to do good to others, even to those who act wickedly against us. We are to seek peace with others, and pursue courses of action calculated to achieve peace. We will not always succeed in being peacemakers, but the failure should not result, even in part, from our own impure and graceless attitudes and actions.

Good relationships require of us hard and consistent work. We must deny ourselves repeatedly; our desires for things great and small must die a thousand deaths. But a self-denying life far from detracting from our blessedness, greatly enhances it. This is because God is always mindful of our ways and prayers. The Lord is for the righteous with his almighty power and inexhaustible blessing (*Rom.* 8:32). Neither need we curse our enemies. If they reject our blessing, it is because they have rejected God's blessing, and remain objects of his holy wrath. Godly blessing never returns to the giver void. For the God who has given us every spiritual blessing in Christ (*Eph.* 1:3), sees to it that what we give to others returns to us purified and multiplied. To know and believe this lightens every load, sweetens every relationship, and fills us with blessed comfort, assurance, and power to continue living according to our holy calling.

17

The Righteous Response to Suffering

And who is there to harm you if you prove zealous for what is good? [14] *But even if you should suffer for the sake of righteousness, you are blessed. And do not fear their intimidation, and do not be troubled,* [15] *but sanctify Christ as Lord in your hearts, always being ready to make a defense to everyone who asks you to give an account for the hope that is in you, yet with gentleness and reverence;* [16] *and keep a good conscience so that in the thing in which you are slandered, those who revile your good behavior in Christ may be put to shame.* [17] *For it is better, if God should will it so, that you suffer for doing what is right rather than for doing what is wrong* (1 Pet. 3:13–17).

As Peter developed his teaching on how believers should live out their faith in their various personal relationships, he touched briefly on the question of how Christians should bear suffering for their faith. In 2:20–25, he wrote of how slaves should bear unjust treatment with patient trust in God, even as Jesus had borne supremely unjust treatment for the salvation of his people. At this point in his letter, Peter returns to the question of Christian suffering, this time explicitly applying his teaching and exhortations to all who stand and serve God by faith in Christ. In particular, our current passage gives practical instruction on how saints are rightly to respond to undeserved persecution. The strikingly simple yet very powerful direction that Peter gives to those who are suffering evil is that they should persist in doing what is good.

THE GOOD POLICY OF GOOD WORKS

The harmonious attitudes and gracious actions detailed previously (verses 8–12) not only please the Lord, whose eyes are on the righteous (verse 12), but also form the best policy as to how we should live in company with our fellow-men. If the Lord is pleased by the gracious lives of his people, then men made in his image, should also appreciate and be pleased by the good works done by the godly.

1. *A zeal for good.* The apostle Paul states the principle that Christians should not pay back evil for evil, but should rather overcome evil with good (*Rom.* 12:17,21). We should resist the temptation to repay in kind what the wicked give to us, because vengeance belongs to the Lord (*Deut.* 32:35). Peter, in these verses, adds that this righteous principle also makes good policy. We should be committed to being good and doing good to all men, not only because God commands it, but also because men tend to commend those who do good.

Peter brings out this point with the rhetorical question of verse 13. In general, even if not in themselves, men condemn such things as lying, stealing, and murdering. At the same time, men approve of honesty and love. If we were to ask any person what sort of neighbours he would choose to have, the answer would not be that he preferred riotous murderers, drunkards, and thieves, but rather people of integrity, who were honest and considerate.

But Peter goes further than simply counselling his readers to do good occasionally so as to avoid arousing men's anger against them. He says that we should prove zealous for all that is good. Ours should not be a merely dutiful resignation to appear good and kind to others. We should jealously guard our attitudes and actions, so that they are ever informed by, and conformed to, that which is good, right, and pleasing to our Lord, as well as by that which is lovingly beneficial to our neighbour. A cultivation of an attitude committed to a consistent performance of good deeds will always serve to prove to sceptics that the saints of God are assets to be appreciated, and not liabilities to be opposed.

2. *Commendation deserved.* Those genuinely zealous for what is good are as lights shining in a dark world. They are different in a way that attracts the admiration of others, as they let the light of God's grace shine forth from them, through their conversation and actions (*Matt.* 5:14-16). Those zealous for good do not pursue the good simply as a policy to placate men. Their aim is always to please the Lord, even when no-one witnesses their actions. Accordingly, when the ways of such believers please the Lord, he makes even their enemies to marvel at them and to be at peace with them (*Prov.* 16:7). Whether those who are zealous for good receive the commendations of men or not, they certainly deserve them.

When Joseph was in Egypt, his commitment to virtuous and godly behaviour won him the respect and confidence of those with whom he had dealings. But he was even more deserving of men's respect and trust than any of those with whom he had contact realized. Potiphar, in fact, punished Joseph because of his wife's unfounded accusations against him (*Gen.* 39:12–20). But Joseph deserved reward rather than jail. He resisted the enticements of Potiphar's wife because of his high regard for Potiphar's propriety, and his higher regard for the Lord.

Joseph was so zealous for good works that he refused to wrong his earthly master and sin against his heavenly Master, though such godly refusal was to bring down man's condemnation upon him.

Joseph was a man truly zealous for good, and he therefore deserved to be promoted by men, not punished by them. Eventually he was so promoted. We, likewise, are called to realize that what God commends in us will ultimately be recognized by men as deserving of their approbation.

SANCTIFIED SUFFERING

The readers of Peter's letter might well have questioned the validity of his assertion in verse 13. The fact is that, however zealous they prove to be for good, Christians do suffer evil from wicked men. The suffering that believers undeniably experience because of loving others and seeking by God's grace to do them good, would seem to call into question the encouragements mentioned in verses 12 and

13. How can the eyes of the Lord be favourably on the righteous, while they yet suffer ill-treatment at the hands of the wicked?

1. *Blessing clothed in sufferings.* Although we are told that if our ways please the Lord, he will make our enemies to be at peace with us (*Prov.* 16:7), Scripture never leads us to believe that obedient believers can avoid all suffering. Men should commend us for our commitment to what is good, but they often perversely hate us and attack us for that commitment. Peter acknowledges this reality in verse 14. Yet, far from teaching that such suffering nullifies the encouragements of verses 12 and 13, he informs us that to suffer for righteousness confirms the great and precious promises of Scripture.

Believers are blessed, even if they do suffer. Jesus tells those so suffering for righteousness' sake that they are to count themselves blessed (*Matt.* 5:10–12). Paul speaks of the sufferings of the faithful producing for them an eternal weight of glory (*2 Cor.* 4:16–18). Suffering does not cancel the blessings of the righteous, it contains them.

2. *Freedom from fear.* When the believer knows and accepts that his suffering for righteousness contains blessing from God, he is set free from fear and agitation. Jesus tells us that while in the world we have tribulation, in him we have peace (*John* 16:33). On numerous occasions during his earthly ministry our Lord told his disciples not to fear (*Matt.* 10:28; *Luke* 12:7; *John* 12:15). Neither are believers to be unsettled by anxiety, a milder form of fear (*Phil.* 4:6, 7). Though the world threatens the children of God, it is the Lord, sitting in the heavens, who laughs the wicked of the world to scorn (*Psa.* 2:1–6). It is not the children of God, but the children of wrath who have great cause to fear the One who sits on heaven's throne, and to dread the wrath of the Lamb of God (*Rev.* 6:15-17). Peter wishes therefore to open the eyes of our faith, so that we might, through the cloud of our suffering, see the blessing that is ours in Christ and the holy retribution that is the lot of those who threaten and try us.

3. *Separation unto Christ.* Rather than spending their time and energies dreading, or trying to avoid or escape, suffering, believers

are called and enabled by God to a more blessed occupation. Christians are to sanctify Christ as Lord in their hearts. We are called to regard Christ as holy and worthy of our reverent fear and our absolute trust. Peter had some practical experiences of both succeeding and failing in this discipline. When he asked Jesus to bid him come to him on the stormy sea, Peter walked on water as did Jesus (*Matt.* 14:25–31). So long as he, by faith, trusted with all his heart in Jesus as Lord over the wind and waves, Peter walked with dominion over the elements. When, however, he regarded the wind and considered it to have mastery, not only over himself, but also over Jesus, he began to sink into the tossing sea.

The psalmist tells of being threatened by the wicked, saying, *The arrogant have forged a lie against me . . .* (*Psa.* 119:69). Yet, rather than being anxiously distracted by their threats, he kept the Lord separated and exalted as the whole focus of his heart and mind, and so was able to declare, . . . *with all my heart I will observe thy precepts.* When, in the days of Daniel, prayer to God was made illegal, Daniel continued to pray to God. Though it led to his being thrown to the lions, Daniel trusted his God as being Lord over the situation, and God exalted him through the trials (*Dan.* 6:7-23). When our triumphant Christ is feared as Sovereign Protector over us, we shall find that we have no other fears (*Isa.* 8:12–13).

4. *Evangelistic consequence.* Men will see us being sustained in our sufferings. They will perceive our hope, however vaguely, and sense the peace we have that passes understanding. Peter, therefore, goes on to say that we should be neither unable nor reluctant to account for the source of our standing even when experiencing fiery furnaces of suffering. We must give our account, however, in the proper spirit. Though the Lord Jesus Christ makes us to be more than conquerors in our tribulations, we must not declare him to others in an imposing, triumphalist fashion. With humble reverence for our Lord's glory, and refusing to take any of it to ourselves, as though we stood by our own power, we are to point men to Christ. With sympathy for the fears and miserable bondage of others, we are to tell them gently of the Saviour, who calls the weary to himself to find rest, and by whose gentleness broken sinners are redeemed and made great (*Psa.* 18:35; *Matt.* 11:28-30).

5. *Guarding the conscience*. We are further told to keep a good conscience in how we stand in our sufferings and in how we tell others about the Lord's sustaining grace and power. Here Peter is telling us to purge our hearts of impure motives. There is a way to tell others about Christ that is intended by the teller to hurt, rather than to heal those who have hurt him. The pure in heart see God (*Matt.* 5:8), and are enabled graciously to stand before men so that men are disarmed and even made ashamed of their maltreatment of believers. To return evil for evil that we have received has never this convicting effect, and it defiles our own conscience with sin.

6. *The will of God*. The blessing we receive in our suffering for righteousness' sake, and the blessing we share with others by a fearless yet gracious witness to Christ, come to us according to the will of God. We should always fear sinning, but never fear suffering. God has ordained our course, including our sufferings, with holy, wise, and loving intention. He disciplines us (*Heb.* 12:3-11), refines us (*1 Pet.* 1:6–7), perfects us in grace (*2 Cor.* 12:7-10), and deepens our loving and holy communion with Christ (*Phil.* 3:10–11). All of this is accomplished through our afflictions, which serve for our sanctification under our Lord's superintendence and through our right response to those afflictions. Thus does suffering become a servant, working for our blessing.

18

Highest Blessing from Deepest Suffering

For Christ also died for sins once for all, the just for the unjust, in order that He might bring us to God, having been put to death in the flesh, but made alive in the spirit; [19] in which also He went and made proclamation to the spirits now in prison, [20] who once were disobedient, when the patience of God kept waiting in the days of Noah, during the construction of the ark, in which a few, that is, eight persons, were brought safely through the water (1 Pet. 3:18–20).

Peter has called upon his readers to suffer for righteousness' sake, and he has connected their sufferings with the will of God (verse 17). To connect the painful and unpleasant call to suffer with the ordaining of the God who is the Saviour of his people and the Lover of their souls can, at first consideration, seem baffling and even repulsive. Rather than encouraging his readers, the apostle's exhortation might well fill them with consternation and questioning as to the wisdom, power, and love of God. The resolution of this painful perplexity is given in these verses. As with all teaching of Scripture, this call for the people of God to endure suffering for righteousness becomes clear on considering the death and resurrection of the Saviour. The cross of Christ ever sweetens the bitterest plight of the believer.

THE PASSION OF CHRIST

In case we think that the call for believers to endure suffering in their determination to do good is unreasonable or despairingly suicidal,

Peter places the call within the context of the passion of Christ. No follower of the Lamb of God will ever face the depths of suffering that Jesus faced. The best Man ever to have lived has suffered the worst things conceivable. Nor was his suffering a meaningless and fruitless tragedy. The highest blessings have resulted from his deepest afflictions.

1. *Supreme suffering.* While believers are called to bear suffering, the Captain of their Salvation bore extensive afflictions that culminated in his death. He suffered not merely annoyance or emotional distress - the most serious form which much of our suffering takes - but he suffered to the ultimate extreme. We do not read that Christ also suffered, as we are called to suffer. We read instead that he suffered unto death. His was supreme suffering, even beyond what some of his people have had to suffer in dying as martyrs for his sake.

2. *Suffering for sins.* We lack the capacity to assess rightly the magnitude and immeasurable depth of Christ's sufferings and death. Our finite and creaturely capacities, clouded as they are by our sin, can never fathom what exquisite pains the perfect Son of God endured in the humiliating and deprived condition of his incarnation. We can but faintly appreciate the burden of shame that he bore, as he who knew no sin became sin (*2 Cor.* 5:21). Still less can we grasp the anguish which he voluntarily experienced in the transaction of our redemption that was finally and fully accomplished on the cross. Christ became a Man and suffered throughout his earthly life, supremely so when he was executed as a convicted criminal and as a blasphemer upon the cursed tree of a Roman cross (*Phil.* 2:5–8). His suffering unto death was unique; it was supreme in its essence, example, and encouragement.

3. *Unfair exchange.* The death of Christ resulted from no natural cause. We sinners have forfeited our lives because we have earned death as the wages of our sin (*Rom.* 6:23). However, Jesus laid down his life voluntarily (*John* 10:15–18). Because he was sinless, death had no claim upon him. However, by divine arrangement which he freely undertook, he submitted himself to death as he exchanged his

perfect righteousness for the unrighteousness of his people. He who was personally sinless was made to be sin, so that in him we might be made the righteousness of God (*2 Cor.* 5:21). A most unfair exchange took place in this transaction; it resulted in his death and our eternal life. Fairness would have necessitated our death and divine condemnation. But by this exchange of the just for the unjust, the magnificent mercy of God has triumphed for us over judgment (*James* 2:13).

4. *Blessed results.* It is understandable when Christians find it perplexing that the God of love wills them at times to suffer for righteousness. That perplexity should be removed when believers consider the passion of Christ and its blessed results. The death of Christ did not result in his destruction, but in our salvation and his exaltation (*Phil.* 2:9–11). As God wills our suffering for wise and loving purposes, and sanctifies us through our afflictions, so also he ordained the saving sufferings of his Son with positive ends in view. The death of Christ was not a random and tragic incident, but a divinely ordered transaction. Through the dereliction and death that Christ suffered on the cross, we who are Christ's redeemed people have been brought near to God. That nearness is one of greatest intimacy. We are accepted by God in his beloved Son. We are adopted by God as his own beloved children (*John* 1:12; *1 John* 3:1).

Peter further adds that Jesus was put to death in the flesh, but made alive in the spirit. By this, the apostle does not mean simply that the physical body of Jesus died while his spirit lived. We are rather to understand that Jesus died in the likeness of sinful flesh and on account of the imputation of our sins to him (*Rom.* 6:10; 8:3). But his death was not his end. He was made alive by virtue of his own perfect and sinless spirit, through which death could maintain no hold on him.

Peter touches upon Christ's death and resurrection in this way to encourage his readers with the truth that through their union with Christ by faith, they, too, have been made to die to sin and to live to God. Read Romans 6:1–11, where Paul works this out in some detail. The point that Peter is making is that through his suffering and death, followed by his resurrection, our Saviour has not only set for us an example but has wrought for us an actual victory over all suffering and even over death and judgment. By faith, believers participate in, and partake of, Christ's victory. It therefore is no longer possible that suffering or death can harm those who are in Christ because, for them, these foes are transformed into servants for their good.

THE PROCLAMATION OF CHRIST

It is difficult to arrive at a dogmatic understanding of Peter's words in verses 19 and 20. It must be acknowledged that confusion and controversy have arisen as students of the Word have endeavoured to grasp and apply his meaning. There have been two main ways in which these verses have been understood in the past. One school of thought asserts that Peter is referring to the pre-incarnate Spirit of Christ who, having anointed Noah, enabled him to preach to the men of his day, whose souls at the time when Peter was writing were in the prison of Hades, or Sheol, awaiting their judgment and sentencing to Hell. The other school of thought is that Christ descended into Hell and proclaimed doom to the unholy angels, particularly those referred to as sons of God in Genesis 6:2, who took to themselves human wives and bred the race of giants who were the Nephilim (*Gen.* 6:4; see also *2 Pet.* 2:4–5).

We cannot enter into the strengths and weaknesses of each of these views in this brief commentary. However, we may say that there is practical and heartening encouragement for suffering saints whichever view is taken of the text. Let us consider the key words and phrases that Peter uses.

1. *In the Spirit*. The words, *in which*, that Peter uses in verse 19 clearly refer back to verse 18 where it was said that Christ was made alive by the Spirit. Thus, Peter appears to have in mind either the pre-incarnate Spirit of Christ, or the post-crucifixion and pre-resurrection Spirit of Christ. We do not need to know which precisely, because both were modes of the being and operation of the Son of God. The holy, divine Spirit of the Son of God has been active through all time, and the perfection of his divinity in union with his humanity made it impossible for death or Hell to hold Jesus.

2. *To the spirits.* The Spirit of Christ made proclamation to *spirits in prison.* Does this mean that his Spirit anointed the preaching of Noah to penetrate to the division of soul and spirit of those held captive to sin's dominion in Noah's day? If so, it teaches us that the preaching of his Word touches all hearers, even those who do not repent, cutting them to the quick, as Stephen's sermon cut the hearts of those who stoned him to death (*Acts* 7:54). Does this mean that Christ harrowed Hell, proclaiming the doom of the fallen, unholy angels, whose dominion was nearly universal in Noah's days? If so, there is comfort for us in the knowledge that by the death of Christ and the accomplishment of our redemption, demonic principalities and powers have been disarmed, and they can no longer dominate those who have been redeemed by Christ (*Col.* 2:15).

3. *Proclamation.* What is clear in these verses is that Christ made *proclamation to spirits*, whether of men or angels. More precisely, he has made proclamation of his victory and of his people's release to both men and angels. His death marks the terminus of sin's power and penalty, and that is good news for men held in sin's thrall. This proclamation has been made by the One who has himself accomplished redemption and destroyed the works of the devil (*1 John* 3:8). He has made it in highest Heaven, on earth, and in the very heart of Hell. The victorious Redeemer has proclaimed that no earthly or hellish fiery furnace has claim to or power over his people.

4. *Days and deliverance of Noah.* Whatever confusion may arise regarding Peter's reference to Christ in the Spirit making proclamation to spirits in prison, the apostle's reference to Noah has clear meaning and application to the scattered and suffering believers to whom he was writing. The passion and proclamation of Christ has wrought salvation for those who trust and obey the Lord. Noah's life typified the trusting obedience of faith, as well as the ensuing salvation of God.

While wicked men and devils are disobedient to God, believers, such as Noah, trust and obey the Lord of salvation. For more than one hundred years, Noah built an ark in preparation for the divine judgment of a flood. There were no indications in Noah's circumstances that such a flood would come. Men were either heedless of Noah's preaching or hostile to it. Yet, for one hundred years, the patriarch laboured by faith in the Word of God.

His fellowship consisted only of seven other members of his own family. But Noah and the faithful few were saved, while the wicked multitude perished. In the same way, the faithful in every age will be saved and vindicated by the God they serve. However greatly they suffer persecution and ridicule from the wicked, and however few they may be, the saints of God will triumph by their participation in the victory of Christ over suffering and death.

19

Holiness and Highest Authority

And corresponding to that, baptism now saves you – not the removal of dirt from the flesh, but an appeal to God for a good conscience – through the resurrection of Jesus Christ, ²² who is at the right hand of God, having gone into heaven, after angels and authorities and powers had been subjected to Him (1 Pet. 3:21–22).

We must bear in mind that what Peter writes in verses 18–22 of this chapter is given as a comforting explanation and incentive for those who were suffering for doing right. The apostle wrote in verse 17 that such suffering was ordained according to the will of God. Those suffering for righteousness might well have questioned why the Lord had ordained such sufferings, and might have wondered what good could possibly issue from their pains. In answer to these practical questions, Peter has reminded us of the sufferings of Christ and the glorious results of his passion. He has mentioned Noah and the suffering that he endured as he prepared for the divine judgment of the flood by building an ark and by preaching righteousness (*2 Pet.* 2:5). In verse 20 he states how Noah and his little family, though they suffered for righteousness, were saved through the universal flood.

We might at first think that it would have been more precise had Peter written that Noah and his family were saved by the ark which bore them safely through the water. However, while that is true and is certainly implied in what Peter writes, the apostle meant to say precisely what he wrote. The waters of God's judgment fell universally upon Noah and all men. But a vital distinction by the grace of God had been interposed between Noah and his wicked contemporaries. The ark saved Noah from the waters of God's judgment, while those waters saved Noah from the reproaches and persecutions of the ungodly, who were destroyed beneath the rising tide of divine judgment.

VIRTUE OF BAPTISM

Peter's mention of Noah's salvation through the awesome divine judgment of the flood, leads him to make personal application to his readers. Each believer addressed by the apostle's words had personally experienced something analogous to Noah's salvation through the waters of divine judgment. Peter draws a correspondence between the saving experience of Noah through the flood waters and that of believers through the water of baptism.

It is not the apostle's intention to draw a correspondence between every detail of Noah's flood waters and of the water of baptism. Rather, Peter seeks to give to suffering Christians a real assurance that they are more safe in Christ, as symbolized by their baptism in the Saviour's name, than was Noah in the ark amidst the purging flood waters of divine judgment.

1. *What baptism is not.* Peter begins with a word of what baptism is not. The sense in which baptism saves is not in its physical application of water to a believer. Baptism is a sacrament wherein by a sensible sign a spiritual grace is conferred by God and apprehended by the faith of those receiving the sacrament. The element, or sensible sign, of baptism is water that cleanses the bodies of all it touches. This outward or physical aspect of baptism is not what Peter means when he refers to its saving virtue.

2. *What baptism is.* The sacrament of baptism has saving power by virtue of its sensible sign and its spiritual reality of which the sign is an emblem. It is not merely the application of water that has saving virtue, but it is the water applied in one's baptism into the name of the Father, Son, and Holy Spirit (*Matt.* 28:19). It is the water of baptism, administered in connection with the Word of God (*Eph.* 5:26) and received by faith on the part of those subjected to baptism,

that saves. This is the true and lasting spiritual cleansing, that makes one a new creature, justified before God, and having a clear conscience before the heavenly Judge. The cleansing agent of baptism is not water, which is but the sensible sign of the rite, but rather the atoning blood of Jesus applied to the believer by God's Holy Spirit (*Heb.* 9:14).

VICTORIOUS RESURRECTION

Such deep, spiritual cleansing of a sinner through the application of the saving atonement of Christ does not leave the sinner sterilized but still spiritually dead. As the flood waters of Noah's day cleansed the earth of the wicked, leaving righteous Noah to live out a new life in a world no longer under the domination of depraved men, so with baptism, the believer is not only spiritually cleansed by the blood of Christ's atoning death, but is also raised up as a new creature, justified in the sight of God.

Baptism signifies our union with Christ in his death and resurrection. Jesus was delivered up to death for our transgressions, and was resurrected for our justification (*Rom.* 4:25). Accordingly, we who have been baptized into Christ, have been baptized into his death, which he died to sin, and we have become united with him in his resurrection, or that new life that he lives to God.

The Apostle Paul draws out this wonderful truth in some detail in Romans 6:1–14. But in our passage, Peter moves quickly from the cleansing of our sins as portrayed in the cleansing water of baptism, to the resurrection and ascension of Christ. He does this so that his readers, who were suffering for righteousness and were being tempted to think that their salvation had little or no real saving power, would realize that by virtue of their union with Christ they were already, in a very real sense, raised up and triumphant over their wicked persecutors.

1. *Highest authority.* Jesus was not only raised from the dead, but he also ascended to the throne of heaven. There our Saviour is seated at the right hand of God. The posture and position of our ascended Lord tells us much about his occupation there and its effect upon his people.

The fact of Christ's session at God's right hand (*Heb.* 1:3) informs us that his work of salvation is accomplished. Unless a man is lazy or exhausted, he sits only when his work is finished. Our salvation is a finished work, having no defects or deficiencies.

The fact that Jesus is at the right hand of God tells us that our Redeemer is in the position of divine honour, power, and authority. The right hand in Scripture is always symbolic of strength. If believers suffer for righteousness, it is certainly not because their Saviour lacks power to protect them, but is rather because there is a holy and loving purpose superintending their afflictions.

2. *Glorious realm.* The place to which Jesus ascended is the very throne of God. It is the place of highest authority and power. That throne is at the heart of the highest and most glorious realm. Jesus reigns in the midst of heaven, which is the highest court wherein only righteous, wise, and loving determinations are made for the redeemed, and righteous and prevailing determinations made against the ungodly. Jesus reigns from the glory of heaven for his people. It is upon this ascended Christ, reigning amidst the glory of heaven, that believers are exhorted to fix their minds and affections, not upon the enticements or intimidations of men on this earth (*Col.* 3:1–4).

3. *His subjects, our servants.* Peter concludes this passage by describing what Christ had accomplished prior to his ascension to heaven. The Saviour did not escape from his wicked enemies by his ascension, leaving his people to contend with them as best they could. Christ subdued all those who are his enemies and the enemies of his people. As in the Book of Esther, wicked Haman, the enemy of the Jews, was hanged on his own gallows that he had built for the hanging of Mordecai (*Esther* 7:10), so all of the Lord's enemies, from the greatest to the least, were defeated and divested of any authority or power over the people of God by the cross of Christ (*Col.* 2:15).

Accordingly, no one can bring a prevailing charge against God's people – not even the subtle accuser of the brethren. Nor can any angel, principality or power, separate us from the love of God in Christ. By his triumphant death, justifying resurrection, and glorious ascension, Jesus has brought us victoriously through all sufferings, all flood waters of divine judgment, and has made us to be more than conquerors with him. By his supreme and sovereign authority, our Lord has reduced all powers, people, and forces to be his subjects, serving for our good (*Rom.* 8:28).

20

Preparing for Productive Pains

Therefore, since Christ has suffered in the flesh, arm yourselves also with the same purpose, because he who has suffered in the flesh has ceased from sin, ²so as to live the rest of the time in the flesh no longer for the lusts of men, but for the will of God. ³ For the time already past is sufficient for you to have carried out the desire of the Gentiles, having pursued a course of sensuality, lusts, drunkenness, carousals, drinking parties and abominable idolatries. ⁴ And in all this, they are surprised that you do not run with them into the same excess of dissipation, and they malign you; ⁵ but they shall give account to Him who is ready to judge the living and the dead. ⁶ For the gospel has for this purpose been preached even to those who are dead, that though they are judged in the flesh as men, they may live in the spirit according to the will of God (1 Pet. 4:1–6).

Persecution was the painful reality and pressing concern of those to whom Peter was writing. While the apostle lovingly sympathized with his readers in their suffering, he offered to them more than sympathy. Peter's opening exhortation of this passage provides the afflicted saints with the substance of encouraging and empowering truths. He reminds his readers that their suffering for righteousness' sake does not indicate that they had been separated from the love, power, and blessing of the Christ whom they worshipped and served. Rather, it is part of the process of bearing fruit for the glory of God and of attaining maturity in the grace of the Lord.

EXHORTED TO ENDURE

Peter reminds his readers that there is the closest connection between the experience of Christ and their own experience. Prior to this passage, he has spoken of the sufferings of Christ (3:18) and of his glorious victory (3:22). He concludes that, since this was the experience of the Head of the Church, then the members of the body of the Church ought to prepare themselves for the same course. The way the Master went sets the way for his servants. It is a way, Peter reminds us, that leads out of degrading sin, through many tribulations, and into the glorious kingdom of God.

1. *Example and victory of Christ.* Since Christ has suffered in the flesh, believers are to prepare themselves for their own suffering in the flesh. The pattern of Christ's earthly life sets the pattern for the earthly pilgrimage of his people.

In the early years of the life of Jesus, he grew in wisdom and stature and in favour with God and men (*Luke* 2:52). In this way, Jesus' life demonstrates the general rule that doing good will usually result in the approbation of men. It was to this rule that Peter referred when he indicated that men, generally, will not seek to harm those who are zealous for what is good (3:13).

However, after the initial popularity of Jesus in the opening year or so of his public ministry, opposition to him increased to the point of his being arrested, tried, and executed as a blaspheming criminal. Our Saviour's supreme suffering for righteousness was according to the predetermined plan of God, as Peter declared in his sermon on the Day of Pentecost (*Acts* 2:22,23). This experience demonstrated that, at times, God's will is that the righteous should suffer (3:17).

These sufferings both of Christ and of his people make sense only in the light of the holy, divine purpose of the Saviour's cross. Christ died for our sins in order to bring us to God (3:18). Our salvation is the good fruit of his suffering. Furthermore, Christ's personal sinlessness and his zeal for doing good – especially the highest good of saving his people – led to his gloriously victorious resurrection (3:21–22).

For the accomplishment of this great and glorious good, the sufferings of Christ were inevitable. That same inevitability holds for all those who are in Christ. Peter touched on this briefly in 1:6, while Paul tells us that all who desire to live godly lives in Christ will be persecuted (*2 Tim.* 3:12). In our passage, however, Peter does not emphasize the inevitability of Christians' suffering so much as the purposeful design and sweet result of that suffering.

2. *Not spectators but participants.* Peter does not draw out the sufferings and glorious victory of Christ as a mere spectacle for believers. Rather, he sets out the humiliating work and glorious exaltation of the Saviour as a pattern in which believers participate. Thus, he calls upon his readers to arm themselves with full and vital knowledge of the truth that Christ suffered and triumphed for his people, not in order to keep them from suffering, but so as to lead them safely and triumphantly through their many tribulations.

The call to spiritual arms is very fitting. Suffering in itself is offensive and painful. It was painful to Christ, as we know from the Gethsemane agonies of his soul. But we must not let the pain stop or dissuade us from a course of doing good as we follow our Saviour. How are we to arm ourselves so that we might endure our sufferings and emerge from them, not defeated or destroyed, but as more than conquerors over them? The answer is that we do this with a right understanding and faithful apprehension of the divine purpose superintending our trials and producing blessed fruits from them.

SWEET FRUITS FROM BITTER SUFFERING

There is always divine purpose in the pains of believers. Peter lists some of God's purposes in ordaining a course of suffering for his people. We contribute greatly to our sanctification when we grasp these divine purposes.

1. *Sinning ceased.* Peter had written in 3:18, that Christ suffered to the point of death. He did this as the sin-bearer for his people (2:24). In the Old Testament, the scapegoat, upon whose head the

high priest laid the sins of the people on the day of atonement, was sent into the wilderness, thus portraying the carrying away of the people's sin (*Lev.* 16:21–22). That pointed to the taking away of his people's sins by Christ, which he did, not by being banished to live in a wilderness with their sins upon him, but by suffering the penalty of those sins. His death made an end of sin's dominion over God's people.

As believers suffer for righteousness, they are to understand that they are not being punished by God for their sins but that they are participating in the sufferings of Christ that freed them from their sins (*2 Cor.* 1:3–7). Though we who believe in Christ have not yet actually died, we are, by faith, to reckon ourselves crucified with Christ (*Rom.* 6:6,7; *Gal.* 2:20). Because of Christ's sufferings, and by every reminder of his sufferings in our own trials, we are to regard ourselves as being as free from sin as though we ourselves had died to sin's power, penalty, and presence (*Rom.* 6:11–13).

2. *Living for God's will.* Our sufferings – most of which are not unto death – are to remind us of our participation in our Saviour's redeeming sufferings and atoning death. However, we are not only freed from sin, but are freed to live according to God's will. Sin had dominated and degraded us; God delivered us from that in Christ and brought us to himself (3:18). Therefore, we who are in Christ do not live as we did when, in our sin, prompted by impure lusts to seek pleasure, we found only pain. We are, instead, informed, enlightened, and empowered by the Word and Spirit of God to live according to the infinitely wise and loving, sovereign will of God. We do this even when God wills that we suffer for doing what is right (3:17).

3. *Deliverance from sinful distractions.* In verse 3, Peter lists a sampling of the sinful endeavours from which his readers had been delivered. The sampling presents a picture of utter abandonment to superficial and transitory pleasures – all of which contain a bitter barb of soul-degrading dissipation. Peter tells us that we have been delivered from that sinfully riotous living, by which sinners seek vainly to silence the convicting voice of God and of their own consciences. The lusts he lists might temporarily deaden those

who indulge in them to the awareness of their sin, but they also deaden them to the vital realities of divine judgment, of heaven and hell, of damnation and, alas, of salvation. Believers have been delivered from such deadening distractions.

SINNERS SEEING AND BEING SEEN

The new life of the redeemed is seen by their old sinful friends. Those remaining in sin assess and make judgments upon their erstwhile friends. In order that believers might not be unduly affected by the judgments of the wicked, Peter briefly reveals how faulty and fatal such judgments are.

1. *Their surprise.* The first thing Peter says about the response of the old associates of believers is that they are surprised that such a change has taken place in their lives. Those dead in trespasses and sin cannot conceive of any reasons to forego the riotous and dissipating carousals that they hope will deaden their sense of emptiness and misery. They are like the Gerasene demoniac, who, before his legion of demons was cast out, was incapable of doing anything except injuring himself and terrorizing others (*Mark* 5:1–15). When such men behold those who used to live riotously with them now living serene, ordered, and godly lives, they are amazed and filled with incredulity that people could actually devote themselves to the will of God rather than to the lusts of men. Their surprise is indicative of sinful blindness and moral stupidity.

2. *Their maligning.* Even more than showing surprise at the new life of the redeemed, sinners reveal their malignant ridicule of them. The wicked judge what they see according to their own guilty and perverted standards. Thus they regard the godly discipline of Christian lives as a dreadful bondage to a fearful Master. They behold the loving devotion that the saving love of God produces in the lives of believers, and regard it as a confining chain that should be cast away rather than welcomed (*Psa.* 2:1–3). In this, the judgment of the wicked fatally fails them.

3. *Their accountability to God.* All the while that the wicked see the new life of the redeemed and ridicule it, they are failing to see something eternally vital. By their riotous living and their ridicule of the godly they are blinding themselves to the truth that their own lives are being seen and judged by the omniscient, living God. Their denial or ignorance of their accountability to the Lord does not reduce that fearful accountability, but increases it by many magnitudes.

LIVING GOSPEL PREACHED TO THE DEAD

What Peter writes in verse 6 is rather difficult and has been subject to various interpretations. We should be guided in our understanding by the context of the verse. In order to console and strengthen the believer under the ridicule of the wicked, Peter has declared that wicked men are themselves accountable to the Christ whom they ridicule, and who shall judge both the living and the dead at his return (verse 5). The word, *for*, with which verse 6 begins in our English versions, connects the verse with the thoughts previously expressed.

Those maligning the Christians were not men who had never heard the gospel. It had been proclaimed to them in their spiritual death, with sincere invitations that they too should partake of eternal life. Furthermore, they had seen the gospel's power in the changed lives of believers. Their rejection of this proffered life and love in Christ served to make their accountability to the Judge of the living and dead that much greater and more dreadful.

No one can escape the judgment of God. Neither those living nor those dead can flee from or avoid giving an account to the divine Judge of all. Christians, too, will be required to give an account of their earthly lives (*2 Cor.* 5:10). But we have an Advocate in Christ, whose propitiatory work for us gives us confidence of acquittal (*1 John* 2:1–6). No amount of earthly suffering can rob us of that blessed confidence, and the taunts of the wicked do but confirm us in godliness, while they add to the guilt with which the wicked shall face the Redeemer, the Judge of all.

21

Serving by Sufficient Grace

The end of all things is at hand; therefore, be of sound judgment and sober spirit for the purpose of prayer. ⁸ Above all, keep fervent in your love for one another, because love covers a multitude of sins. ⁹ Be hospitable to one another without complaint. ¹⁰ As each one has received a special gift, employ it in serving one another, as good stewards of the manifold grace of God. ¹¹ Whoever speaks, let him speak, as it were, the utterances of God; whoever serves, let him do so as by the strength which God supplies; so that in all things God may be glorified through Jesus Christ, to whom belongs the glory and dominion forever and ever. Amen (1 Pet. 4:7–11).

P eter has exhorted his readers in 4:1–6 to bear suffering patiently. In this present passage, the apostle further exhorts his readers not to endure these persecutions passively, but to fulfil the will of God actively within the furnace of their afflictions. Those who live in the Spirit according to the will of God are ever active, rendering service for the glory of God and the good of their brethren, even in seasons of trial.

ULTIMATE PERSPECTIVE

The apostle has already encouraged his readers to view their sufferings from the perspective of being united to Christ in his saving work. He has appealed to them to understand that as the afflictions of Jesus accomplished incalculable good for the glory of God and for his people, so also our sufferings will have a blessed issue in the end. Having called upon us to consider the accomplishment of redemption in the past, Peter now extends his call by exhorting us to look toward the future consummation of redemption in glory. He points his readers to the truth that they live by faith with respect to both the cross and the crown.

When Peter says that the end of all things is at hand, he is not teaching that in his own day the return of Christ was imminent. Had he been declaring that, he would obviously have been wrong. We should understand that he is not speaking in terms of time, but in terms of the accomplishment of our salvation. Regarding that accomplishment, there remains nothing left for the Lord to do. The work is finished, and its full fruition in glory is as certain as if it were immediately upon us. By faith we apprehend this, and thus any present period of suffering is perceived as being but momentary (*2 Cor.* 4:17). Therefore, Peter exhorts us not to live as though the oppressions, deprivations, and persecutions of this age were permanent. Rather, these afflictions are virtually over, and the day of the judgment of God, when it comes, will show to all how temporary and transitory the powers of this world have been throughout history. This is the true and ultimate perspective from which the apostle would have his suffering readers view their momentary, light afflictions. From this perspective, they will not merely endure their painful circumstances, but will rise up by the enabling grace of God to be productive for the good of others and for the glory of God.

1. *Sound judgment.* Those living in vital awareness of the final day of divine judgment and righteous disposal of all things should themselves maintain and live by sound judgment. By this, Peter means that we should think all matters through with minds transformed by the Spirit's application to us of the saving mercies of God in Christ (*Rom.* 12:1–2). Thus, we are called to exercise godly discernment, to think in the light of God's Word, so as to arrive at true assessments of all the situations we encounter. Soundness of judgment also implies an integrity and compatibility between our own thinking and the mind of the Lord, as expressed in the whole counsel of God. Thus Peter calls us to yield up our minds captive to Christ, so that we think, speak, and act in conformity with God's

will. Sound judgment is not like the thinking of the fool who leaves God, his Word, and his saving works out of his consideration (*Psa.* 10:4; 14:1; 53:1). A man exercising sound judgment maintains the priority of seeking first the kingdom of God and conforming his life to God's righteousness (*Matt.* 6:33).

2. *Sobriety.* The exercise of sound, godly judgment leads one to live a sober life. Biblical sobriety is not to be equated with gloomy morbidity, nor is it that glib and giddy attitude that some mistakenly call the joy of the Lord. The sober man thinks clearly and feels rightly in all situations. He rejoices with those who rejoice in the Lord; he weeps sympathetically with those who are sorrowful (*Rom.* 12:15).

Specifically, Peter calls upon his suffering readers to maintain sobriety amidst their afflictions just as Jesus retained his clarity of mind when on the cross he refused the sour wine offered to him as a dulling intoxicant (*Mark* 27:34). The apostle exhorts his readers not to dull their sense of suffering through their pursuit of carnal distractions (2:11), but rather to be quickened by the reading of God's Word and by the illumination of his Spirit. In the light of his Word, we see the rich resources we have in Christ and the high and privileged responsibilities that are ours as servants of the Lord.

3. *Prayer.* To cultivate sound judgment and sobriety is a necessary prerequisite for performing our supreme duty, highest responsibility and greatest privilege, namely, prayer. The discipline of prayer heads the list of our duties in Christ. This is so because prayer is the efficient means by which we desire and accomplish everything in our walk with Christ. Prayer is the enlightening and empowering foundation for fulfilling all that Peter will exhort us to do in verses 8 and 11. Yet, prayer is more than the energizing force enabling us to do the will of God. It is our means of communion with Christ. It is the response of the soul to the saving grace of the Lord. By prayer, we devote ourselves to our Redeemer before we launch into service for him. The reversal of that priority can result only in a degeneration of devotion into a dutiful resentment that neither pleases the Lord nor blesses our brethren. Read how Martha, the practical sister of the more pious Mary, had to learn this lesson from Jesus (*Luke* 10:38–42).

FULL EMPLOYMENT IN THE FAMILY OF FAITH

Instead of encouraging his readers to concentrate upon their suffering, with resulting paralysis or hysterical questing for temporary relief, Peter leads them to higher, better ground. He guides them from the liberating and prayerful contemplation of the cross and the crown to the call of their Christian duty. This call to the performance of duty in Christ is not meant as a distraction of his readers from their sufferings. It is rather a call to enter fully into the true career of every believer. Paradoxically, those who know that the end of all things is at hand live most responsibly in the days before that final day. It is those who are most heavenly minded who are of most earthly use.

As we give ourselves to minister to our brethren, we find the pains of our sufferings diminished. We also find that what we thought to be the impediment of our afflictions is no prison prohibiting us from the free exercise of our loving service. In Christ, our suffering does not preclude our service, but promotes it. There is no such thing as unemployment in Christ's kingdom. If we have sound judgment and sobriety enabling us rightly to pray to our God, we shall find that he calls and empowers us to know and to do his will even in the most adverse of circumstances.

1. *Loving the brethren.* Our prayers to God always lead us to relate lovingly to all men, especially to our brethren in Christ. Therefore, Peter exhorts his readers to make their priority the maintaining of fervent love for one another. Such love is the queen of all virtues; the chief aspect of the fruit of the Spirit (*Gal.* 5:22). Holy love is at the heart of God's law, as Jesus makes plain when he summarizes the law as loving God with all our powers and our neighbour as ourselves (*Mark* 12:30–31).

We do well to note that Peter does not tell us to manufacture or to begin the exercise of love for our brethren in Christ. This is so because all who are in Christ have been loved by the Father, and so have the divine love to share with others (*1 John* 4:19). The wicked may deprive believers of many things, but not of the love of God in Christ that we possess and pour out upon our brethren.

Our love for one another is not to be a cold and heartless outward performance, but rather is to be fervent. With vital warmth, holy passion, and sacrificial extravagance, we are to lavish our loving thoughts, words, and deeds upon our brothers and sisters in Christ.

The transforming power of this love is touched upon when Peter writes that love covers a multitude of sins. Here we learn that the love of which Peter writes is not like that self-regarding desire that the world calls love. The unregenerate must see something desirable in another person to love that person. Godly love does not discover but deposits loveliness in another. Christian love is not put off by the faults and sins of the brethren. Such love leads us to expect to find sins in others, but then leads us further to the right eradication of those sins. It is not that our love covers the sins of others by ignoring them. That would be as ineffectual as Adam trying to cover his nakedness with a fig leaf. Instead, love regards the sins of brethren as being cleansed by Christ's blood, and covered with his righteousness. Furthermore, the love of Christ for us covers with healing balm the wounds that the sins of our brethren have caused in us. We should therefore guard and cultivate this healing and restoring power of love.

2. *Hospitality*. Peter gives a representative, not an exhaustive, list of Christian duties in verses 8 to 11. When he obliges his readers to practise hospitality, he calls them to a most practical exercise of love, one well suited to minister to the suffering, scattered aliens to whom he was writing. He urges this exercise of grace not only upon those who were married and had capacious houses. He who multiplied fish and loaves is the One who called us by his apostle to exercise hospitality, and he can and will stretch our fare.

Christian hospitality is more than food and comfortable accommodation. It is a domestic offering of fellowship in Christ. The blessing of offering our homes as an environment for the exercise of love for the brethren is emphasized when Peter tells us to be hospitable without complaint – as though giving such practical love was impoverishing, rather than enriching. Once again, poor Martha exemplifies the believer who, by complaining, made Jesus a judge in her home, rather than a beloved guest.

3. *Gifts received to be given.* As it is with love, so it is with all other spiritual gifts and graces. We do not manufacture what we are called by God to share with others. We render our service according to the gracious supply of God (*Phil.* 4:19). Whether our gifts are those that involve speaking or serving, we are to recognize that we have received a rich, divine supply to be used for the blessing of others in the body of Christ.

Peter tells those with word gifts to speak the utterances of God. By this, he does not mean that we proclaim inspired revelation, but rather that we are to engage in sanctified conversation in which the truth is uttered in love, and we endeavour to turn all conversations to things godly and excellent. The apostle directs those with work gifts to be gracious doers of the Word and will of God. Such workers labour by the strength God supplies, and by that strength they do not grow weary in well doing but mount up with wings like eagles, soaring to ever greater heights of loving service.

GOD GLORIFIED

It would be quite natural for those suffering, as were the readers of Peter's letter, to complain of their plight as powerless victims. However, Peter views them as soldiers of Christ and issues marching orders for those who, as more than conquerors, are enabled by the grace of God to rise up from their afflictions and render service for Christ. As Peter's own mother-in-law rose from her fever to wait on Jesus and his disciples immediately after our Lord healed her (*Mark* 1:30,31), so we are called to rise above our afflictions to do by grace that which redounds to the glory of God, who lavishes his enabling grace upon us. We are called and equipped to serve and shine with a supernatural light that will glorify the divine Giver.

22

Reviling, Rejoicing and Revelation

Beloved, do not be surprised at the fiery ordeal among you, which comes upon you for your testing, as though some strange thing were happening to you; ^{13} but to the degree that you share the sufferings of Christ, keep on rejoicing; so that also at the revelation of His glory, you may rejoice with exultation. ^{14} If you are reviled for the name of Christ, you are blessed, because the Spirit of glory and of God rests upon you (1 Pet. 4:12–14).

Peter continues to write about suffering for righteousness. He has concentrated on this theme in 1:6; 2:20–25; and 3:14–4:6. In the present passage, the apostle employs repetition with conscious design. He does so in order to counter the waves of suffering his readers were enduring with waves of truth emphatically proclaimed. Each time Peter treats the theme of our suffering for doing good in Christ's name, he advances our understanding of the reality that our suffering is in union with Christ and has a glorious, not a shameful or destructive, purpose.

REALITY OF THE SAINTS' SUFFERING

Peter has already in this letter acknowledged with sympathetic understanding the reality of what believers suffer as a consequence of working out their faith in love. He continues to acknowledge that grim reality in this passage. He does not understate the ferocity of the attacks launched by the wicked against the righteous. When he compares the sufferings of his readers to a *fiery ordeal*, he is acknowledging fully the painful and potentially consuming nature of their trials. Yet, just as there was a great, unseen reality of angelic hosts surrounding the seen reality of that Syrian army sent to seize the prophet Elisha (2 *Kings* 6:15–17) – a prevailing reality apprehended only by faith – so there is more to the reality of our sufferings in and for Christ than can be perceived by natural sense. It is both the seen and unseen realities that Peter sets before us when he writes of the saints' suffering.

1. *Fiery ordeal.* Peter admits, as he refers to his readers' sufferings as a *fiery ordeal*, that there was nothing mild and easy about what they were enduring. Their afflictions were to them as painful as burning fire; as fierce as a consuming blaze, stoked by hellish fiends. This painful reality threatened to consume the thoughts and energies, if not the lives, of those enduring it.

The apostle is sympathetically concerned with their very real pain. But he is even more concerned with the purpose and final result of their fiery ordeal, and he writes to lift his readers to this higher consideration. Fire may be destructive, but when something as precious as gold is thrust into it, the precious essence is refined while the impurities are burned away.

It is this purifying purpose that guides the afflictions of believers. As when Daniel's friends were thrown into the fiery furnace, there to experience closer fellowship with the Son of Man, while losing the cords binding them (*Dan.* 3:23–27), so also all the fiery ordeals to which believers are subjected serve to purify and strengthen their faithful grasp of Christ and enhance the security they enjoy by a closer, more vital fellowship with him.

2. *Testing.* That our refinement and not our destruction is the design of our sufferings is implied in the word Peter uses that is translated, *fiery ordeal.*

The ordeal may be painful, but it has divine purpose for our ultimate good. The higher purpose superintending the painful ordeal is made explicit when Peter goes on to say that such ordeals come upon us for our *testing.* A wild fire simply burns, but a testing fire has a positive, refining design. A testing fire also has a wise and controlling hand superintending the test, insuring that what goes into the furnace, being precious and enduring, emerges from the refining flames in greater purity and value.

In the opening verses of this letter, Peter spoke of this testing process for refining our faith (1:6,7). In the present passage, the apostle's teaching has advanced to the point where he instructs us that, by the ordaining wisdom of God, sufferings refine our characters. Peter well knew what he was writing about. He himself had experienced suffering at the hands of Satan. By the prayers of Jesus, the satanic temptation was transformed into a testing that had not only refined Peter's faith, but had sifted his very character, separating the chaff of sin from the fine wheat of his new nature in Christ (*Luke* 22:31–32).

3. *Sharing the Saviour's sufferings.* The sufferings of the Christian produce such high and blessed ends because the believer who suffers for righteousness does not suffer alone but always in union with Christ. Peter therefore speaks of his readers *sharing the sufferings of Christ.* He does not mean by this that our sufferings have an atoning value as did those of our Redeemer; still less are our sufferings penal, for the Saviour has borne the full penalty of our sins for us. What is meant by sharing Christ's sufferings is that through our union with Christ, our sufferings become productive of good, as his sufferings were productive of glory.

Daniel's friends suffered a literal fiery furnace because of their faithfulness to their Lord (*Dan.* 3). In their crucible of affliction, they discovered that their Redeemer was with them. He who would bear the sins of all his people, and the consequent painful penalty of those sins, who endured the flames of hell to deliver his people from that eternal burning, was with Daniel's friends. He caused Nebuchadnezzer's blazing furnace to be not only safe, but also sanctifying, for the servants of God. So it will prove for all believers who share in the productive sufferings of the Redeemer.

4. *Blessed.* The apparent reality, when believers suffer for Christ's sake, is that they are abandoned, if not cursed, by the hand of God. But Peter reminds us that we are *blessed* by God if we are reviled by man for the name of Christ. Even such painful persecution is part of that which God causes to work together for good (*Rom.* 8:28).

When we suffer for Christ, the good wrought in this life is the refinement of our faith and the sanctifying of our characters, and after this life it is an inconceivably great reward for us in heaven (*Matt.* 5:10–12).

5. *Beloved.* The apparent reality, when believers suffer for Christ's sake, is that they are neglected, if not hated by God. By affectionately referring to them as *beloved*, Peter reminds us and them that the reality encompassing believers is that they ever possess the love of their brethren, such as Peter himself, and are ever embraced by the immeasurable and unchangeable love of God. That Peter points to the hand of our loving heavenly Father, superintending our trials, should be to us a most fortifying comfort, as apples of gold in settings of silver.

OUR RESPONSE TO OUR SUFFERING

The Word of God surrounds each soul suffering for Christ with fortifying light and loving consolation. Through Peter's teaching concerning the nature of trials, we learn that our pains are purposeful and productive. An application to ourselves of this truth should condition and control our response to any suffering for Christ. Rather than being shocked and ashamed by our persecutions, we should find cause to rejoice in them.

1. *Nothing strange or surprising.* That the world should hate, revile, and persecute us for our devotion to Christ and for our demonstration of his love, might easily seem to us a strange thing. We might expect a more welcoming response to our demonstration of the love of God in Christ. However, when we bear in mind the hatred of the world against the Lord and his Anointed (*Psa.* 2) and the infernal malice that Satan and his devils bear against those who are in Christ (*Rev.* 12), we should expect and prepare for the ungrateful attacks of worldly men against us when we seek to publish abroad the saving grace of the gospel.

When we rightly understand how God presses our sufferings into his holy and loving purposes, rendering them servants for our good, we are also inclined not to be surprised, but rather to expect persecutions. Armed with such expectation, we learn to regard our afflictions not as disturbing strangers, but as expected agents ministering for our advancement in grace (*2 Cor.* 12:7–10).

Nor are we to be surprised by our fiery ordeals. Peter himself was surprised when Jesus announced for the first time that he would suffer and die at the hands of his enemies (*Matt.* 16:21–22). He was surprised in the courtyard of the high priest, when a servant-girl identified him as one who had been with Jesus (*Mark* 14:66–67). He was surprised because he refused to believe that his suffering for Christ was anything other than a strange and unendurable thing to be avoided at all costs, even the cost of denying Jesus three times. In contrast, Peter in the Book of Acts is as bold as a lion, when he and John, in response to the threats of the Sanhedrin forbidding them to teach in the name of Jesus, declare: *We must obey God rather than men* (*Acts* 5:27–29). At this point in his letter, Peter is appealing to his readers not to be as he was, in regarding his suffering for Christ as an unendurable surprise, but to be as he had become, expecting and enduring fiery ordeals for God's glory and for his own good.

2. *Not shame but glory.* Wicked men revile those who trust and obey Christ. Peter instructs believers not to feel ashamed because of such reviling, as though they were guilty of some great wrong. Our Lord Jesus Christ was reviled, mocked, and abused at his trial and upon the cross. Yet, as Peter himself proclaimed in his Pentecost sermon, the Jews were not crucifying a shameful criminal, but the One whom God had made to be both Lord and Christ (*Acts* 2:36). Paul agrees, writing that had the rulers of this age really known the wisdom and perceived the glory of God in Christ, they never would have crucified him (*1 Cor.* 2:8). For Christians, the reviling of men against them for their trust in Christ is indicative of the ignorant guilt of the revilers. It indicates also the just destruction towards which the taunting of those who are the apple of God's eye justly hastens such mockers (*Phil.* 1:28).

While the wicked revile Christians, the rich reward of God rests upon them. The glorious Holy Spirit dwells in them. The illuminating and empowering Spirit ministers comfort to suffering believers, giving them assurance that their afflictions are but momentary, their sufferings light, and that what they endure for Christ's sake is producing for them an eternal weight of glory (*2 Cor.* 4:16–18). God also rewards his suffering people by manifesting himself to them, through his Word and Spirit, with special intimacy. There is nothing quite like walking through the valley of the shadow of death to convince us that our Lord is with us indeed, resting his hand of sustaining power and rewarding provision lovingly upon us.

3. *Rejoicing.* Since our Lord has a blessedly productive purpose, a lovingly superintending hand, and a glorious reward for us in and through our sufferings, our response to sufferings should be rejoicing (*Matt.* 5:11, 12). We have the strongest reason to rejoice in the knowledge that nothing can separate us from the love of God in Christ, and in the reality that in Christ we are, like him, made more than conquerors in all things (*Rom.* 8:37–39). We should rejoice in the Lord's special nearness to us in our fiery afflictions. The sure hope of glory that we have, together with the knowledge that our sufferings are not worthy to be compared to that glory, should fill us with grateful rejoicing (*Rom.* 8:18).

Though our glory in Christ may be hidden now from the eyes of the reviling world, and even at times clouded from our own vision, we possess in Christ a glory that by faith can presently be glimpsed, and that should inspire joy in us. The fullness and perfection of that glory we will behold by sight at the revelation of our glorious Redeemer, in whom now our lives are hidden until that final day of revelation and surpassing joy (*Col.* 3:3,4).

23

Suffering and Service

*By no means let any of you suffer as a murderer, or thief, or evil
doer, or a troublesome meddler;* [16] *but if anyone suffers as a
Christian, let him not feel ashamed, but in that name let him
glorify God.* [17] *For it is time for judgment to begin with the
household of God; and if it begins with us first, what will be the
outcome for those who do not obey the gospel of God?* [18] *And if it
is with difficulty that the righteous is saved, what will become of
the godless man and the sinner?* [19] *Therefore, let those also who
suffer according to the will of God entrust their souls to a faithful
Creator in doing what is right* (1 Pet. 4:15–19).

Peter has written much about Christian suffering in this letter.
There was a pressing and practical need for him to develop this
theme. The Roman emperor, Nero, was soon to begin serious
persecution of Christians throughout the Empire. The apostle of the
Suffering Servant of God strives therefore to prepare his readers for
the tide of afflictions that was rising against them. However, Peter
would have his readers understand that there was a right and a wrong
way for those who bore the name of Christ to suffer. He writes
therefore, in this passage, of the kind of suffering that believers
should avoid and the kind of suffering they should embrace.

SUFFERING TO AVOID

Not all suffering has a sanctifying effect upon the sufferer. Crimes,
for example, bring the suffering of punishment upon those who
commit them. Peter exhorts his readers to avoid that kind of

suffering, and to do so by their faithful determination to avoid the crimes that are the roots of such bitter fruits. The apostle lists some representative crimes that would have had special significance for those living under the increasing pressure of persecution. His readers would very likely have found themselves pressured to retaliate in some way against their persecutors, thinking themselves so justified by necessity that their loving and sympathetic Lord would understand, even if he would not approve. Peter emphasizes that by no means should anyone bearing the name of Christ resort to criminal behaviour.

1. *Murderer*. It might seem incredible to us that any Christian should consider, let alone commit, the act of taking another's life. Such extreme retaliation against their persecutors would have accomplished nothing for suffering Christians except make them guilty of breaking the sixth commandment of God, and rendering them criminals amongst men. Their arrest, trial, conviction and punishment would then be just. Homicide would not relieve believers from persecution, but would involve them in transgression against God and make them subject to judicial punishment at the hands of the civil authorities.

2. *Thief*. Christians are no more to take another's property than to take another's life. Stealing from those who unjustly persecuted them might have seemed, for the original recipients of this letter, a fitting way for them to gain some compensation from their persecutors. However, thieves are also sinners against God and criminals amongst men, rightly deserving their punishment.

3. *Evil doer*. Peter adds to the specific crimes of murder and stealing a general term that covers all other criminal offences. The evil doer is one who launches sinful thoughts into actions that violate the law of God and the civil statutes of man. Any who practise such bad deeds are precisely those whom Paul, in his Roman epistle, says should be punished by the civil magistrate (*Rom.* 13:3–4).

4. *Meddler*. One who meddles in the affairs of others may not be committing a crime, but he does deserve to receive some sort of

social censure. Some commentators suggest that this term applies to political agitators, whose seditious activities deserve criminal punishment. Whatever form such disturbances of the public peace and welfare might take, Peter clearly teaches that no Christian should be guilty of such crimes, and thus become subject to their penalties.

SUFFERING TO EMBRACE

There is, however, a form of suffering that the believer is to embrace, should it come upon him. Ultimately, under Nero, it became a punishable crime simply to be a Christian. There may have already been local statutes against Christianity in some of the provinces where Peter's original readers lived. If, therefore, the so-called crime were that of a person being a disciple of Christ, Peter encourages his readers not to bemoan their conviction but rather to boast in it.

It would naturally unsettle those committed to fulfilling God's commandment to love one's neighbour, if they were being thought of by their neighbours as violators of man's law, simply because they sought to walk according to the statutes of the Lord. Yet Peter tells those who are suffering for being Christians not to feel ashamed. So long as they could maintain a clear conscience before God (3:16), they had no real cause to bow their heads in shame before any man. Indeed, Peter tells his readers that they should boast in the name of Christ, and glorify the God who had wrought for them such a great salvation. No civil punishment could ever deprive them of their heavenly citizenship, nor could any sinful wrath of man separate them from the love of their heavenly Father.

THE VERDICT OF GOD

From his discussion of how Christians should and should not suffer under the verdicts of men, Peter proceeds to discuss the far more significant judgments and verdicts of God. In this way, the faithful apostle follows the instruction of his Saviour, who told his disciples not to fear those who could only kill the body, but rather to fear God, who is able to destroy both body and soul in hell (*Matt.* 10:28).

1. *The household and the gospel of God.* Most English versions of verse 17 read as though Peter is saying that the sufferings of Christians for righteousness' sake are, in fact, a judgment of God sent upon the Church. The implication is that such divinely ordained judgments purge the Church of false believers, while refining true children of God. This may be the meaning Peter intends, in which case, believers are to be heartened by the knowledge that their righteous and loving heavenly Father superintends all the afflictions that befall his people. The suffering saints should be further encouraged by knowing that although such judgment begins with them, and serves for their good, it does not end with them, but rather proceeds to the unbelieving world. With this understanding, persecuted believers could be assured that their persecutors would not be allowed to escape from having to give an account to God for their wicked hounding of his Church.

Yet, the original language suggests that Peter's specific intention in verse 17 is slightly different from that expressed above. Literally, the verse reads: *For the time is for judgment to begin from the household of God.* This reading suggests that Peter wishes his readers to remember that their persecutors were storing up righteous, divine wrath to be poured upon them in the day of judgment, precisely because they had maltreated the living stones of God's habitation. Furthermore, Peter refers to the growing guilt of those persecuting the church when he writes that they do not obey the gospel of God. It is sinfully wrong for men to attack the people of God. Doing so is considered by God an attack upon himself. Jesus did not ask of Saul of Tarsus: *Why do you persecute Christians?* Rather, the Lord confronted that persecuting Pharisee with the words: *Why are you persecuting Me? (Acts* 9:4). The people of God are imperfect in this life, and thus their faults may be magnified by godless men as an excuse to attack the saints. But the gospel is perfect, true, and gloriously good news. Those rejecting it are judged already, the divine verdict against them being that they have not believed in the name of the only begotten Son of God (*John* 3:18).

2. *Saints and sinners.* In verse 18, Peter quotes Proverbs 11:31 to emphasize that the saints have no cause to envy their sinful persecutors, or to harbour resentment and indignation over the

apparently free hand that the wicked have in persecuting them. As Asaph testifies in Psalm 73, the righteous have no cause to envy the godless, for the Lord has already placed the feet of the wicked on the inexorably slippery slope of his just condemnation (*Psa.* 73:18–20). The challenges and difficulties of believers are but temporary scaffolding, used to produce for them an eternal weight of glory (*2 Cor.* 4:16–18). The comforts and wicked caprices of the godless form a millstone around their necks, irresistibly dragging them to the eternal torments they so richly deserve.

TRUST AND OBEDIENCE

Peter concludes his teaching on the painful subject of Christian suffering with a final exhortation in verse 19. The apostle issues an exhortation that believers should not only endure their afflictions passively, but positively entrust their welfare in time and eternity to God.

1. *The will of God.* Throughout this letter, Peter has stressed that Christians who suffer for righteousness' sake do so not apart from but because of the ordaining hand of God (3:17). It is a deeply fortifying encouragement when we know that the infinite wisdom, the immeasurable love, and the holy will of God work in concert to accomplish his glory and our blessing, through the things we suffer for his name's sake. It should console all suffering saints to know that by means of their afflictions, their prayers, in which they ask that God's will be done on earth as in heaven, are being truly answered.

2. *Entrusting to God.* The pain of our suffering, whatever its cause, can impose upon us a determination to escape the suffering at all costs. However, when we are taught that our suffering for Christ is according to God's will, we are led to endure affliction, not by a passive resignation, but by an active entrusting of ourselves to God. The word translated *entrust* has the connotation of delivering a treasure to a securing agent for safe-keeping. In this case, we entrust the treasure of our immortal souls to God, whom Peter designates *a faithful Creator.* The agent securing us is the Creator and Sustainer of our lives and of the lives of our enemies. He is the divine Sovereign,

who governs all for our good (*Rom.* 8:28). He is faithful to his covenant promises never to leave or forsake us, but ever to deliver us from all threats, alarms, and enemies. The entrusting to which we are called is modelled upon the entrusting of our Saviour, which led ultimately to his victorious triumph over sin, death, and judgment (2:20–23).

3. *Enacting good.* Our trust in God is to be enacted in our behaviour towards men. We are to do good even to our enemies (*Luke* 6:28). We are not to strike at our enemies, as Peter did when he cut off the ear of the high priest's slave at the arrest of Jesus (*John* 18:10–11). Our suffering does not justify our becoming evil doers (verse 15), seeking to live by the arm of flesh and wielding the tools of this perishing world. We live and prevail by trusting our Saviour, and we honour him by doing good to all men in his Name.

24

Exemplary Elders

Therefore, I exhort the elders among you, as your fellow elder and witness of the sufferings of Christ, and a partaker also of the glory that is to be revealed, [2] shepherd the flock of God among you, exercising oversight not under compulsion, but voluntarily, according to the will of God; and not for sordid gain, but with eagerness; [3] nor yet as lording it over those allotted to your charge, but proving to be examples to the flock. [4] And when the Chief Shepherd appears, you will receive the unfading crown of glory (1 Pet. 5:1–4).

The reality of the faith of believers sinks or swims when the tide of their suffering for that faith rises. Peter has been teaching believers how to endure their sufferings and how to grow as their faith is exercised in the furnace of affliction. In sum, he has told them to entrust the welfare of their souls to their faithful God and to remain committed to doing what is right. Such a trusting of the wise and loving God who tests his people is the foundation for all the service which believers render when they return good for evil. It is certainly the basis for the service to which elders in the church of the Lord Jesus Christ are called. So Peter proceeds from the general exhortation of 4:19 to a more specific exhortation addressed to elders.

THE ELDERS ADDRESSED

It is those called and equipped by God to lead their brethren as they trust and serve the Lord that Peter addresses as he begins to draw his letter to its close. The elders to whom he writes are exhorted to render exemplary service as they fulfil their office. The Lord would not have novices or the half-hearted to lead his people. From Peter's exhortation we learn something of the responsibilities of elders, so that those who are elders might know what God expects of them, and so that members of the churches might know both what to expect from and how to pray for their elders.

1. *The office.* The term used by Peter and which our English versions translate, *elders*, has the basic meaning of maturity in terms of chronological age. When he uses this term in contrast with that of younger men, mentioned in verse 5, we might conclude that the apostle is issuing an appeal to all the older members of the churches to whom he is writing. However, elsewhere in Scripture, the term, *elder*, clearly refers to the ecclesiastical office devoted to the ministry of the Word and prayer (*1 Tim.* 3:1–7; *Titus* 1:5–9). Those serving in the office of elder are to possess and exercise such qualities as wisdom and gravity that usually accompany the attainment of mature age. They are especially to possess and exercise those spiritual gifts and graces that Scripture sets as requirements for the office. Our Lord's good and wise care of his people is manifested by the necessity taught in his Word that those who lead his Church should be mature in grace and competent in the gifts of leadership.

2. *Plurality.* Peter does not address a single man, but rather a plurality of men serving in the office of elder. It is true that the apostle was writing to scattered aliens, addressing several churches and therefore, possibly, a collection of elders, one from each assembly. Yet, consistently in Scripture, we find elders serving together in local congregations to give spiritual leadership (*Titus* 1:5), and representing their congregations at general assemblies and councils composed of commissioners from local churches, in order to decide matters of faith and practice (*Acts* 15:1–6, especially verse 6). The Word of God that tells us there is wisdom among many counsellors (*Prov.* 11:14) also informs us that the officers of Christ's church should serve as a company of elders, leading the flock with their accumulated wisdom.

THE ELDER ADDRESSING

This exhortation for elders rightly to shepherd the flock of God under their care, is being given by Peter. He was among the twelve disciples of Jesus, and part of the inner circle of the disciples closest to Jesus (that is, Peter, James, and John). He was also an apostle. Yet he uses none of these special designations as he addresses his readers. We note from this how humble the previously proud disciple had become through the sanctifying work of the Lord.

1. *Fellow-elder.* The term Peter employs to describe himself as he addresses the elders amongst his readers is *fellow-elder.* He does not claim any primacy over these church officers to whom he was writing. He emphasizes, rather, the point that he too holds the office to which they had been ordained. Peter was writing as one who served with his fellow-workers in the churches of Christ. We discover here the principle of parity amongst elders, wherein there is an essential equality of authority, responsibility, and power in all who hold that office. Peter is not writing as a primate, ordering his underlings, but he appeals rather to those ordained by the calling of the Lord to the same office as himself.

2. *Singular witness.* To the office of elder which he shared with his fellow-elders, the apostle adds something that he did not have in common with them. Peter reminds his readers that he was an eye-witness of the sufferings of Christ. He does not boast as a fellow-sufferer with Christ, but he acknowledges that he had been made to see and to accept those sufferings of the Saviour which at one time he had considered unthinkable.

When, at Caesarea Philippi, Jesus disclosed to his disciples that he would suffer and be killed at Jerusalem, Peter declared: *God forbid it, Lord*. But by the time he wrote this letter Peter had not only seen Jesus suffer, but had come to understand and accept how essential those sufferings were for the salvation of God's people. He had come to embrace the atoning sufferings of his Saviour. Indeed, we may rightly say that Peter boasted in those saving afflictions of Jesus, as is indicated by his numerous references to the sufferings of Christ in this letter (see also 1:11, 18, 19, 21; 2:21–24; 3:18; 4:1, 13). Much comfort would have been brought to these suffering saints, including the elders to whom Peter was writing, by their being reminded that they suffered in union with Christ, and that his sufferings ended not in defeat and death, but in triumphant resurrection and ascension to glory.

3. *Fellow-partaker of glory*. Neither the sufferings of Christ, nor those of his people, are goals in themselves. Both for Christ, and for the believer, suffering begets glory (*Luke* 24:26; *Rom.* 8:17; *2 Cor.* 4:16–18). Therefore Peter goes on to refer to himself as a *partaker*, along with his readers in general and his fellow-elders in particular, of the glory to come. He is himself a partaker of glory, not a contemplator of it nor a lecturer about it. He also refers to the glory to be revealed, indicating that we possess that glory essentially and certainly now in its reserved form, apprehended by faith, prior to its full disclosure in us (*Rom.* 8:18). This reference to glory is given so as to raise the thoughts of the elders addressed to a right contemplation of their high and holy calling, and remind them of the immeasurable privilege and honour they possess as holders of the office.

THE EXHORTATION

The substance of Peter's exhortation to his fellow-elders is found in verses 2 and 3. In it, Peter is not ordering, requesting, or even suggesting, things to his fellow-elders. He is rather appealing to them most forcefully to heed his words.

1. *Its character*. The literal meaning of the word translated, *exhort*, in verse 1 is to call to one's side. An exhortation, therefore, is not an order so much as a strong appeal, calculated to persuade those receiving it to come to the position of the one issuing it.

Peter exhorts his fellow-elders to shepherd the flock of God. It is, essentially, a call that Peter himself received from Jesus after his resurrection, when he was restored to service from the sin of having denied his Lord three times (*John* 21:15–17). The call to shepherd the flock involves elders in feeding, guarding, guiding, and protecting those otherwise vulnerable to starvation, attack, wandering, and injury. Elders are not called to entertain God's people, by pandering to their misguided desires for ear-tickling and superficial fare (*2 Tim.* 4:1–5). They are called to a serious, sacrificial, and vital ministry. The flock they shepherd is precious beyond reckoning, having been purchased by the blood of God's Son (*Acts* 20:28).

2. *Attitude of service.* The weighty responsibility of the elders' calling, coupled with the fact that they are often unappreciated, if not opposed, by the sheep they seek to shepherd, can become a heavy burden. Therefore, Peter addresses the temptation that elders may have to view their calling wrongly or to abuse their office. By three negations, with their positive correctives, the apostle delineates the right attitude by which all elders should serve in their office.

The first negation is issued against an attitude of dutiful drudgery. Elders are not to serve as reluctant leaders, compelled into service by the overpowering hand of God. They are rather to serve with diligence and delight, sensing the privilege of their high office and the abundant provision that God has made for their success in it by his enlightening Word and enabling Spirit.

The second negation is against self-gratification. Peter exhorts elders not to serve for sordid gain. These officers are not to be motivated by the thought that their office exists for their own material prosperity or for their self-aggrandizement. Instead, they are to be eager to treat members of the flock as more important than themselves, promoting them to higher honour and blessing by feeding them with the Bread of heaven (*Phil.* 2:3).

The final negation prohibits an imperious attitude and commends leadership by way of humble, grateful, and exemplary service. By this third aspect prescribed by Peter, elders are reminded that those in their charge have been allotted to them by the Chief Shepherd of the sheep, who will require of them an accounting for the souls under their care (*Heb.* 13:17).

3. *Incentive for service.* The implicit reference in verse 3 to the Lord under whom elders render their service becomes explicit in verse 4. Those called to shepherd the flock of God are reminded that they serve by the direction and through the enabling power of the Chief Shepherd of the flock. Whatever suffering and sacrifice elders

must bear in the faithful performance of their duties, they are to know that they serve by the gracious provision and for the glory of their Lord, the Good Shepherd who laid down his life for his sheep.

This Chief Shepherd is not distant from the elders of his church. Peter therefore does not refer to his coming, but rather to his appearing. When the Chief Shepherd does appear, he will richly reward the service of his elders. Whatever cost they bore in the course of their faithful shepherding of the flock, Christ will infinitely repay with an enduring crown of glory. No higher incentive could motivate the Lord's servants than the prospect of receiving their divine Master's commendation: *Well done, good and faithful servant. Enter into the joy of your Master* (*Matt.* 25:21).

25

Exaltation through Humility

You younger men, likewise, be subject to your elders; and all of you, clothe yourselves with humility toward one another, for God is opposed to the proud, but gives grace to the humble. ⁶ Humble yourselves, therefore, under the mighty hand of God, that He may exalt you at the proper time, ⁷ casting all your anxiety upon Him, because He cares for you (1 Pet. 5:5–7).

Peter has exhorted elders to shepherd the flock of believers entrusted to their care by Jesus, the Chief Shepherd. Elders in the Church of the Lord Jesus are to lead by being examples of Christlikeness. However, it is not only elders who are exhorted, but the members themselves are also encouraged to follow the edifying lead of their elders.

SUBJECTION TO SUPERIORS

There is a right and holy order in the body of Christ. Jesus himself speaks of those who are the greatest and least in the kingdom of God (*Matt.* 5:19; 18:4). Accordingly, Jesus has appointed officers to lead his people on earth, and that is why Peter has exhorted elders to lead the flock in a worthy way. Contained in that exhortation is a call for elders to lead by giving examples of humble submission to the Chief Shepherd (verse 4). In the present passage, the apostle calls for all believers to respect and live in subjection to their spiritual superiors.

1. *Age and office.* We have noted that the term, *elders*, as Peter employs it in verses 1–4, does not refer so much to chronological

age as to the office of spiritual leadership in the Church. However, in verse 5, Peter specifically exhorts the younger men to subject themselves to their elders. Here the age factor is clearly under consideration. Quite certainly, the young men addressed are not officers or a class within the churches, but just men who are of a young age. These are exhorted to subject themselves not only to those who are older than themselves, but specifically to their spiritual elders, who are called and equipped by God to serve as their edifying leaders and examples.

There is great wisdom in Peter's focus upon young men in this exhortation. For youths tend to be those least inclined to subject themselves humbly to others, even their superiors. Young men are often driven to exert themselves, and are least likely to sense the need to listen to and learn from their elders. The apostle, therefore, singles out those most inclined to follow their own strong passions, rather than godly principles, and tells them plainly to exercise humility and subject themselves to their wise, considerate, and spiritually capable elders.

2. *Your elders.* Those to whom Peter tells young believing men in particular, and other members of the Church in general, to subject themselves, are their own elders. The apostle does not commend his readers mindlessly to follow strangers or tyrants who would impose themselves upon the flock. The elders of a congregation are those who have been recognized and duly elected by the congregation to serve as spiritual leaders. As such, elders are due all the loving respect and obedient support to which their office entitles them.

Furthermore, elders are charged to feed, guide, and protect those under their care. The elders of Christ's Church are called and equipped to keep watch over the souls of the flock, and to do so as men knowing that they must one day give an account to the Lord for the fulfilment of their charge (*Heb.* 13:17). We should note the wise and loving provision of our Lord in this arrangement. Elders are to serve joyfully and humbly in their charge; members are to submit cheerfully and gratefully to their elders, whose highest concern is for the spiritual welfare of those members. Christ gives a blessed and fruitful harmony to his church.

PRACTICE OF HUMILITY

From a call to young men to submit to their elders, Peter proceeds to extend a call to all his readers to practise humility. They are to do this not simply in subjection to their elders, but also in their relationships to one another.

1. *Call to all Christians.* The call to practise humility is one issued to all who name the name of Christ. It is essentially a call for us to practise grace and love in all our dealings with one another. Paul, in his letter to the Philippians, issues the same call when he tells us to regard others in the body of Christ as being more important than ourselves (*Phil.* 2:1–4).

When Peter writes that we should clothe ourselves with humility, he is not telling us to be hypocritical actors, pretending to be humble when really we are not. What the clothing image is intended to convey to us is the understanding that our first impulse or our natural feelings should not be regarded as right and loving. Humility is never natural to a sinner, and even as redeemed people we still have sinful tendencies. So Peter tells us to reflect upon our attitudes and actions towards others in the Church, and to adopt the very mind of Christ as our own (*Phil.* 2:5).

2. *Conformity to the Lord.* The exhortation that we clothe ourselves *with humility* is really an exhortation for us to put on the Lord Jesus Christ and make no provision for our sinful, selfish flesh (*Rom.* 13:14). Jesus declares himself to be meek and humble in heart (*Matt.* 11:29). He is the source of humility and self-sacrifice. He assumed the role of a servant; indeed, of a criminal, pouring out his life for us so that we might have eternal life. The Son of God humbled himself because he delighted to serve his heavenly Father, who had himself determined to save sinners, though it cost him infinitely to do so. God is therefore opposed to all who, in their sinful pride, act as though they do not need to receive this exquisite gift attained by the self-sacrificial humility of the Son of God.

3. *Self-control.* Peter's call for his readers to clothe themselves *with humility* is a call for them to exercise the gifts and graces of their new

nature in Christ. It is a call that can only rightly be obeyed willingly and voluntarily. We see this in the active imperatives the apostle uses as he tells us to clothe ourselves and to humble ourselves. We are not to wait for God to humble us by his faithful and loving hand of chastisement directed against our pride. The call is to place ourselves in the lower place, the place of costly service to others, from where we deal with them as though they were more important than ourselves.

BLESSING OF HUMILITY

This call for us to humble ourselves and to honour others before ourselves may seem like a call to a performance of a grim, impoverishing duty. However, we learn from Peter that godly submission is not a form of degrading slavery. Nor is humility some kind of curse that confines us to the lowest place.

1. *The exalting hand of God.* The One under whom we humble ourselves is God. It would seem that assuming a servant's place before the King of Glory would confirm us in that lowly position, for who can rise above the divine hand under which we humble ourselves? Paradoxically, however, we learn that our highest blessing comes to us as we humble ourselves under the hand of God. This is because the desire of God's heart is to give grace to the humble. God's hand is ever at work therefore, not in pressing down the lowly, but in lifting them up.

The petty and tenuous heights that we can attain by our own proud efforts cannot compare with the towering peaks of enduring glory to which the hand of our God will exalt us. He who raised his Son, the suffering Servant of Israel, from the grave, taking him up to sit in heaven's glory at his right hand, giving him a name above every name, will not fail to exalt all who in Christ die to selfish ambition and determine humbly to serve their God.

We must note, however, that God does not necessarily exalt immediately those who humble themselves under his hand. Peter informs us that it is at the right or proper time that God exalts the humble. Joseph endured his trials in Egypt for more than twenty years before he was exalted by God to rule over Pharaoh's realm.

Jesus lay in the tomb for three days before he was raised by God from the dead. Thus, we must learn to exercise patience as we await the full and exalting blessing of God upon our humbling of ourselves.

2. *Our casting, God's caring.* God's delay in exalting the humble is because, in his perfect wisdom and power, he waits to bring it about at the best time for his glory and our good. Therefore, the patience that we must exercise while we wait for the Lord's response should be filled with trusting contentment and grateful hope. We also have the blessed assurance that we need not be crushed under the burdens we undertake, in our determination to render humble service to others for Christ's sake. The casting away of our pride brings with it the immediate blessing of being invited to cast away all our burdens of fear and anxiety. This blessing is unlimited for Peter tells us to cast all our anxieties upon the Lord. Those who humble themselves under God's hand do so not in proud self-reliance but with a trusting reliance upon the capability of God to tend to their burdens with a competence infinitely greater than their own.

This casting of our anxieties upon the Lord is no careless abandoning of responsibilities or a faithless presumption upon God. It is our Lord himself who invites us by his Word and Spirit to come to him for relief from our burdens (*Matt.* 11:28–29), and to let our prayerful requests to him vanquish all anxiety in us (*Phil.* 4:6–7). Peter tells us that the God on whom we cast our burdens and worries deals with them with far greater care and competence than we could ever do.

He also tells us something even more wonderful than that God bears our burdens. He insists that the reason God replaces the anxieties we cast upon him with his peace that passes understanding, is that he cares for us. We have a caring God, who regards us as precious in his sight and beloved in his heart. Our Lord cares for our burdens more responsibly than we could care for them. He cares for us, however, even more than for the burdens we cast upon him. Our God watches over our welfare infinitely more than we could ever do. As we go down into true humility, we go ever more deeply into the relieving care and loving exaltation of God. As the truly humble have ever discovered and testified, the way up for the Christian is down.

26

Resistance and Relief

Be of sober spirit, be on the alert. Your adversary, the devil, prowls about like a roaring lion, seeking someone to devour. ⁹ But resist him, firm in your faith, knowing that the same experiences of suffering are being accomplished by your brethren who are in the world. ¹⁰ And after you have suffered for a little while, the God of all grace, who called you to His eternal glory in Christ, will Himself perfect, confirm, strengthen and establish you.¹¹ To Him be dominion forever and ever. Amen (1 Pet. 5:8–11).

The Word of God tells us that we do not wrestle against flesh and blood, but against great, unseen, spiritual enemies (*Eph.* 6:12). The scattered and suffering believers to whom Peter was writing were well aware of their human persecutors. In these verses, the apostle draws back the curtain of sensual perception to reveal the spiritual kingpin of evil, who ever orchestrates the malice of men against the Church of Christ. The teaching of God's Word does not only reveal the devil to us, but also provides effective measures for us to prevail against his demonic attacks.

CALLED TO VIGILANCE

Having just called us to humility in our Christian living and service (verses 5–7), Peter now teaches us that vigilance is necessary for prevailing in spiritual warfare. The enticements and intimidations of Satan are unavoidable. No believer can elude or escape him, nor is any follower of the Lord exempt from the wiles of the devil. What

Peter teaches in this passage is not so much how to avoid our great, unseen spiritual foe, but how to stand against his evil onslaughts.

1. *Carefree, not careless.* It is instructive for us to note that this call to spiritual vigilance follows immediately upon the call to cast all our anxieties upon our caring God. Our being freed from all worrying cares might be misconstrued, so that we might think we can live our Christian lives in a heedless, careless way.

The truth is that although the Lord Jesus calls us to himself to receive rest for our souls, he also calls us to bear his easy yoke and light burden (*Matt.* 11:28–29). The rest that we receive from our Redeemer results from his lifting of the crushing burden of our sin, with all its miserable consequences. The yoke of the Lord refers to the diligent service to others to which he calls us, and for which he equips us. It also refers to our union with him in his priorities; to our guidance by him by means of his revealed will; and to our enabling by his gracious provision. Therefore, there is no contradiction between the fact that our Lord bears our cares and the fact that he calls us to a careful walk as we endure the attacks of Satan. We may think that we cannot find rest, peace, or security so long as the enemy of our souls lives to afflict us. But God makes his triumphant provision for us in the face of this enemy (*Psa.* 23:5). Our Lord provides for us the very spiritual armour he himself wore in his victory over Satan (*Isa.* 59:15–17; *Eph.* 6:10–18). It is as we carefully apply to ourselves this divine provision that we experience continued freedom from fear and anxiety, and we enjoy peace that passes understanding.

2. *Sobriety.* Peter defines what he means by vigilance under two headings. The first heading is sobriety, and it is negative. The second heading is alertness, and it is positive. The apostle has already in this letter called his readers to be sober (1:13). Here again, he exhorts us to arouse ourselves from those distractions that intoxicate our spiritual senses, making them dull in perception and slow in response. Such things as the fearful burdens mentioned in verse 7, and the carnal allurements mentioned in 2:11 can smother our spiritual vitality, giving Satan an advantage over us, and the Lord would arouse us from such a state.

3. *Alertness.* When Peter tells his readers to be on the alert, he is speaking of the positive action of a sober saint. Our attention should be high, and focused on our Saviour, and on all that he tells us in his Word. Part of what Jesus tells us is that his followers should expect and prepare for spiritual battles against Satan. In the Olivet Discourse, recorded in Mark 13, Jesus repeatedly warns his disciples to be watchful (verse 5), to be on guard (verse 9), to take heed (verses 23, 33), and to be on the alert (verses 33, 35, 37).

If our faith is rightly fixed on Jesus, he will direct us so that we keep an eye on Satan and do not fall for his wiles. Our security is not undermined by such spiritual alertness, but enhanced by it. The Christian in his watchfulness against Satan exemplifies the attitude commended by the Russian proverb about history, which says: *He who keeps an eye on the past, loses an eye; but he who does not keep an eye on the past, loses both eyes.*

RESISTING THE ENEMY

Peter has shown his readers that their main concern should be more to resist sin rather than to avoid suffering. From the consideration of indwelling sin and pride, the apostle turns his readers' attention to the person of Satan, the exploiter of the sins of believers, whose deceptive wiles lay snares for the saints so that they fall into sin. Peter offers some brief but very incisive and practical teaching on the nature of the devil, how he acts, and how we can prevail against him.

1. *Who he is.* Peter refers to our great spiritual enemy as our *adversary*. It should be our settled understanding that Satan is always against us. Because he is a liar however, he often approaches us as a friend and good counsellor. In Genesis 3, the devil posed as one interested in the highest welfare of our first parents, telling them that it was God who wished to keep them lowly and dependent, while he wished to exalt them to the status of God (*Gen.* 3:5). Even though Satan can appear to us as an angel of light (*2 Cor.* 11:14), it is vital that we always remember that he is our adversary, and that he is at his most dangerous when his advice and devices appear to be for us.

Peter also refers to our enemy as *the devil*. This word literally means someone who trips others up by throwing something between their moving legs. Satan does not prefer to wrestle with diligent Christians, for he knows that if he comes into the grasp of the sons and daughters of Jacob – the patriarch who wrestled with God and prevailed – he will be defeated. Instead, the devil prefers to throw some accusation against us to discourage us, or to hurl some tempting thought or troubling fear at us, so that we stumble and lose our standing in the Lord.

2. *How he acts.* Peter describes our great spiritual adversary's methods when he tells us that the devil *prowls about*. Scripture consistently portrays Satan as restless and on the move (*Job* 1:7; 2:2). He may not be near us today, but with stealth he seeks an opportune time to draw near to us, pouncing upon us with his fiery darts when we least expect him.

The fact that Peter represents Satan as *a roaring lion* should alert us to the fact that the devil is hungry for the ruin of souls, and this is why he is ever on the prowl. Male lions roar when they are hungry, and their roaring summons the females to hunt for food. Satan ever roars with a gnawing emptiness driving him to desperate attempts to find satisfaction in our destruction.

That the devil aims at nothing less than our destruction is emphasized when Peter writes that Satan is *seeking someone to devour*. The devil does not intend to annoy or wound us only. He aims deadly missiles at our heads and hearts, seeking to darken our thinking and depress our feelings so that we succumb to despair. It would be better for us if the devil were a lion, rather than merely like a lion. The comparison drawn does not exaggerate our enemy's prowess when it likens him to a fierce, subtle, and destructive lion. The devil is far worse than any earthly lion!

3. *Resistant faith.* This passage not only draws a lurid and sobering portrait of the devil, but also teaches us how we may prevail against such an awful foe. The apostle does not provide for us an arsenal full of all types of weapons. Instead, he points us to the single resource that alone can vanquish this enemy. We are called to resist the devil, firm in our faith. There are many ways we can avoid, escape from,

trap, chase away, or kill a lion. But there is only one effective tactic we can use against the devil. From Satan we can neither run nor hide; we cannot reason with the devil; nor appeal to his mercy; nor buy him off. We must stand against him united to our victorious Lord by faith. Read Ephesians 6:10–18 on this point, noting in that passage how Paul repeatedly calls upon his readers to stand firm against the devil in the evil day (*Eph.* 6:11, 13, 14). Exercising the faith that God has given to us, by which we are united to Christ in his victory over all the works of the devil (*1 John* 3:8), will not only sustain us, but will also compel Satan to flee from us (*James* 4:7). For by faith not only perceive the prowling lion, but we behold and cleave to the Lion of Judah who has overcome the devil for us (*Rev.* 5:5).

CONSOLATION OF VIGILANCE

Being called to spiritual vigilance is not a grim necessity of the Christian life, but part of our blessed pilgrimage by grace to glory. God makes sinless use of Satan's sinful attacks against us. We grow in trusting gratitude to God as we find his provision to be more than adequate in enabling us to persevere and prevail in our spiritual battles. We also draw nearer to our brethren when we find ourselves under common attack. There is great divine consolation for us in the fires of spiritual combat.

1. *Shared suffering.* We should be encouraged to know that we are not singular victims of the devil's attacks, but serve rather as a glorious band of brethren in a great and supremely significant spiritual war. Peter not only tells us that we share the experience of the devil's attacks with our brethren, who are also targets of the evil one; he also informs us that these painful spiritual conflicts accomplish something. We do not merely endure our sufferings, but our experience of them accomplishes many wonderful things for God's glory and our good.

2. *Limited suffering.* Relief is added to encouragement when we read that our spiritual conflicts have limited duration. Peter tells us that we must suffer only for a little while. The enticements and intimidations of Satan may seem to us, when we are in their midst,

to have no end. But they are limited, not by Satan's mercy, but by God's will. As God limited the afflictions Satan could heap upon Job, telling the devil that he had to spare Job's life (*Job* 2:6), so our Lord sets an end to our sufferings. It is most instructive for us to note, however, that even had God not set a limit to Job's sufferings, the faith of Job would have made him more than conqueror still. For Job declared that even if God should slay him, he would still trust his Lord (*Job* 13:15). This perspective of faith makes the duration of our sufferings to be seen as but a little while and as producing for us an eternal weight of glory (*2 Cor.* 4:16–18).

3. *Sanctifying suffering*. Peter concludes this passage with words of supreme consolation. He speaks of *the God of all grace who called us to his eternal glory*. These magnificent truths remind all who suffer in Christ that the grace of God is at the beginning of their course of spiritual conflicts, sustaining them until they reach the end to which he has effectually called them, namely, his eternal glory. We can prevail against the devil because our God himself perfects us, despite Satan's accusations; he confirms and strengthens us by his grace; and establishes us in his glorious presence blameless and with great joy (*Jude* 24). Our God will not let us fail or fall in our contests with Satan. For it is neither persecuting men nor the prowling devil who have dominion over the lives of those in Christ. It is the God of grace and glory who has dominion in our darkest days as well as in the days of light. We stand by, and in, the God who has dominion over all things through all time and eternity.

27

Gracious Final Greetings

Through Silvanus, our faithful brother (for so I regard him), I have written to you briefly, exhorting and testifying that this is the true grace of God. Stand firm in it! She who is in Babylon, chosen together with you, sends you greetings, and so does my son, Mark. Greet one another with a kiss of love. Peace be to you all who are in Christ (1 Pet. 5:12–14).

Amidst the anguish of his readers' suffering and the painful necessities of spiritual warfare, Peter concludes his letter with loving greetings. In Christ, spiritual toughness does not diminish loving tenderness. Indeed, it is the tender mercies of the Lord, ministered amongst the members of Christ's body, that fortify the saints for the spiritual battles they must endure.

GREETINGS FROM BRETHREN

Peter wrote in verse 9 that the same experiences of suffering which his readers were facing were being experienced by their brethren throughout the world. With these final greetings, the apostle conveys to his readers a final encouragement of loving communion with some of their fellow sufferers and soldiers in Christ. Jesus had taught his disciples that the world would hate them (*John* 15:18–19), and those to whom Peter was writing were experiencing this. But a far greater truth than the reality of the world's hatred was the fact that these suffering saints were loved by their brethren, who prayed for them and sent them their greetings.

1. *Silvanus*. Peter first notes that Silvanus was the penman, or scribe, of this letter, though Peter himself was its author. This incidental acknowledgement seems to account for the fine Greek style of the letter, in comparison with the more rough style of 2 Peter, probably written by the apostle's own hand. More significantly, Silvanus is regarded and commended by Peter as his faithful brother. From some of Paul's letters, we gather that Silvanus was a faithful co-labourer of his, along with Timothy (*2 Cor.* 1:19; *1 Thess.* 1:1; *2 Thess.* 1:1). Whether he served with Paul or Peter, Silvanus was a faithful worker and a loving brother because he was, first and foremost, faithful to his Lord. Peter mentions no greetings from Silvanus, probably because Silvanus would deliver this letter and add his own personal greetings.

2. *She who is in Babylon*. The apostle refers to the church in Rome, of which he was the pastor, under the figure of a woman in Babylon. The woman is the local church, a part of the bride of Christ. Her members lived, worked, and worshipped in the capital city of the empire. But when Peter refers to Rome as Babylon, he is reminding his readers that they should never envy their brethren because they lived in the great metropolis, with its economic, social, and cultural wealth, and its majestic imperial splendour. In reality, Rome was a painted harlot (*Rev.* 18), and her spirit was as oppressively set against the Christians of Peter's day as had been the spirit and armies of the Babylon of old against the Jews they carried away into captivity.

It is a testimony to the sustaining power of the exhortations found in this letter that there were still saints to be found in pagan Rome. They were being increasingly castigated and condemned by the imperial might, but were chosen, beloved, and preserved by God, and sent their loving greetings to their similarly chosen brethren in Asia Minor (1:1). They who dwelt in Babylon were not of Babylon, but were, like the brethren they greeted, aliens and strangers in this world (2:11).

3. *Mark*. Just as Paul had a spiritual son in Timothy (*1 Tim.* 1:2), so Peter had a spiritual son in Mark. In contrast with the stalwart faithfulness of Silvanus however, Mark was a man who had failed in his faithfulness to Christ. He had deserted Paul and Barnabas whilst

on mission with them, and had occasioned a serious, if not sinful, separation between Paul and Barnabas (*Acts* 15:37–40). With Mark and Peter it was a case of like father, like son, in that Peter himself had failed badly when he denied Jesus three times. But these two men were trophies of the Lord's restoring grace, just as Silvanus was a trophy of God's sustaining grace. No child of the Lord's saving grace would receive anything but a welcomed ministration of the fortifying grace and love of Christ in any greeting sent to them from either Peter or Mark.

GRACE FROM GOD

Whether the men sending their greetings to the recipients of this letter were faithful soldiers, like Silvanus, or enticed and oppressed but enduring saints, like the members of the Roman church, or fallen yet restored servants, like Peter and Mark, all of them were what they were by the saving grace of God. They all stood and served together for the glory of God and for the good of their beloved brethren by God's grace.

1. *Standing in grace.* Peter and his co-labourers and fellow-believers in Rome did not experience the manifold grace of God, and then keep it to themselves. The apostle has written, *briefly* but sufficiently, in order to share this grace with his readers. Firstly, with those in Asia Minor, but afterwards with all the readers of this letter throughout the ages. Nor does the apostle merely declare this grace; he exhorts his readers to *stand firm in it*. We stand against suffering, sin, and Satan, only as we faithfully and firmly adhere to the grace of God. We must never be contented with hearing and heeding the grace of God, as contained in his Word, in a vague, indeterminate way. We should hunger and thirst to know, to be, and faithfully to do, all that our gracious God conveys to us.

2. *Shared love.* The greetings Peter would have believers exchange with each other are to be more than mere words. The apostle encourages his readers, therefore, to express their loving greetings in holy, tactile gestures, such as a chaste kiss. We should ever embrace one another in Christ with loving salutations, encouraging each

other to love and good works by the holy intimacy fostered in our fellowships.

3. *Securing peace.* The *true grace of God* that Peter mentions in verse 12 reconciles us in love to God and to man. The fruit of that grace working itself out in love is peace with God and with our brethren (1:2). That grace also gives us peace that passes understanding as we work out our salvation in the world and within our furnaces of affliction. As Peter himself had repeatedly experienced the peace that Jesus works in the heart – whether walking on stormy waters (*Matt.* 14:29) or being restored by his gracious Lord on the shore of the Sea of Tiberias after he had repeatedly denied him (*John* 21:1–19) – so he would have all his readers to experience Christ's peace, even amidst tribulation. This subjective peace is grounded in the objective peace that Jesus accomplished between God and man by his death on the cross. It is the felicitous security that the believer has in knowing that whatever storms he faces in the world, the God of heaven is at peace with him, graciously accepting him in his beloved Son.

This grace of God is the alpha of salvation, producing peace in our hearts throughout our earthly pilgrimage, until it ripens into its omega of eternal glory. Whatever trials men and devils may bring upon Christians, we do well never to forget that it is by such grace and for such glory that God has chosen us in Christ.

Group Study Guide

SCHEME FOR GROUP BIBLE STUDY
(Covering 13 Weeks)

Study Passage	Chapters
1. 1 Peter 1:1–5	1–2
2. 1 Peter 1:6–12	3–4
3. 1 Peter 1:13–25	5–7
4. 1 Peter 2:1–8	8–9
5. 1 Peter 2:9–12	10–11
6. 1 Peter 2:13–20	12–13
7. 1 Peter 2:21–3:7	14–15
8. 1 Peter 3:8–17	16–17
9. 1 Peter 3:18–22	18–19
10. 1 Peter 4:1–11	20–21
11. 1 Peter 4:12–19	22–23
12. 1 Peter 5:1–7	24–25
13. 1 Peter 5:8–14	26–27

This Study Guide has been prepared for group Bible study, but it can also be used individually. Those who use it on their own may find it helpful to keep a note of their responses in a notebook.

The way in which group Bible studies are led can greatly enhance their value. A well-conducted study will appear as though it has been easy to lead, but that is usually because the leader has worked hard and planned well. Clear aims are essential.

AIMS

In all Bible study, individual or corporate, we have several aims:

1. To gain an understanding of the original meaning of the particular passage of Scripture;
2. To apply this to ourselves and our own situation;
3. To develop some specific ways of putting the biblical teaching into practice.

2 Timothy 3:16–17 provides a helpful structure. Paul says that Scripture is useful for:

(i)   teaching us;
(ii) rebuking us;
(iii) correcting, or changing us;
(iv) training us in righteousness.

Consequently, in studying any passage of Scripture, we should always have in mind these questions:

What does this passage teach us (about God, ourselves, etc.)?

Does it rebuke us in some way?

How can its teaching transform us?

What equipment does it give us for serving Christ?

In fact, these four questions alone would provide a safe guide in any Bible study.

PRINCIPLES

In group Bible study we meet in order to learn about God's Word and ways 'with all the saints' (*Eph.* 3:18). But our own experience, as well as Scripture, tells us that the saints are not always what they *are* called to be in every situation – including group Bible study! Leaders ordinarily have to work hard and prepare well if the work of the group is to be spiritually profitable. The following guidelines for leaders may help to make this a reality.

Group Study Guide

Preparation:

1. Study and understand the passage yourself. The better prepared and more sure of the direction of the study you are, the more likely it is that the group will have a beneficial and enjoyable study.
Ask: What are the main things this passage is saying? How can this be made clear? This is not the same question as the more common 'What does this passage "say to you"?', which expects a reaction rather than an exposition of the passage. Be clear about that distinction yourself, and work at making it clear in the group study.

2. On the basis of your own study form a clear idea *before* the group meets of (i) the main theme(s) of the passage which should be opened out for discussion, and (ii) some general conclusions the group ought to reach as a result of the study. Here the questions which arise from 2 Timothy 3:16–17 should act as our guide.

3. The guidelines and questions which follow may help to provide a general framework for each discussion; leaders should use them as starting places which can be further developed. It is usually helpful to have a specific goal or theme in mind for group discussion, and one is suggested for each study. But even more important than tracing a single theme is understanding the teaching and the implications of the passage.

Leading the Group:

1. Announce the passage and theme for the study, and begin with prayer. In group studies it may be helpful to invite a different person to lead in prayer each time you meet.

2. Introduce the passage and theme, briefly reminding people of its outline and highlighting the content of each subsidiary section.

3. Lead the group through the discussion questions. Use your own if you are comfortable in doing so; those provided may be used, developing them with your own points. As discussion proceeds, continue to encourage the group first of all to discuss the significance of the passage (teaching) and only then its application (meaning for us). It may be helpful to write important points and applications on a board by way of summary as well as visual aid.

4. At the end of each meeting, remind members of the group of their assignments for the next meeting, and encourage them to come prepared. Be sufficiently prepared as the leader to give specific assignments to individuals, or even couples or groups, to come with specific contributions.

5. Remember that you are the leader of the group! Encourage clear contributions, and do not be embarrassed to ask someone to explain what they have said more fully or to help them to do so ('Do you mean . . . ?').

Most groups include the 'over-talkative', the 'over-silent' and the 'red-herring raisers'! Leaders must control the first, encourage the second and redirect the third! Each leader will develop his or her own most natural way of doing that; but it will be helpful to think out what that is before the occasion arises! The first two groups can be helped by some judicious direction of questions to specific individuals or even groups (*e.g.* 'Jane, you know something about this from personal experience . . .'); the third by redirecting the discussion to the passage itself ('That is an interesting point, but isn't it true that this passage really concentrates on . . . ?'). It may be helpful to break the group up into smaller groups sometimes, giving each subgroup specific points to discuss and to report back on. A wise arranging of these smaller groups may also help each member to participate.

More important than any techniques we may develop is the help of the Spirit enabling us to understand and to apply the Scriptures. Have and encourage a humble, prayerful spirit.

6. Keep faith with the schedule; it is better that some of the group wished the study could have been longer than that others are inconvenienced by it stretching beyond the time limits set.

7. Close in prayer. As time permits, spend the closing minutes in corporate prayer, encouraging the group to apply what they have learned in praise and thanks, intercession and petition.

NOTE: Though the Study Guide which follows is arranged in thirteen studies, each contains enough material for it to be divided into two studies, making a programme of twenty-six studies in all.

Group Study Guide

STUDY 1: 1 Peter 1:1–5

AIM: To understand something about the character and circumstances of the writer of this letter and its readers.

1.   The author of this letter was named Simon, the son of John. How did he come to have the name, *Peter*, and what is the significance of the change in his name? (see *Mark* 3:16; *John* 1:42).

2.   What practical comforts would the first readers of this letter derive as Peter addressed them as the chosen people of God? What comforts would we today have in knowing that we are similarly chosen of God?

3.   What is the connection between *grace* and *peace*, and what practical meaning would there be for these readers as Peter invoked upon them these blessings in fullest measure?

4.   What does it mean when Peter writes, *Blessed be the God and Father of our Lord Jesus Christ*?

5.   Compare and contrast our merit and God's mercy, in the context of our salvation.

6.   Why does Peter use negative terms, such as *imperishable* and *undefiled* and *unfading* when he describes the believer's inheritance?

7.   What does it mean that believers are *protected by God's power through faith*?

FOR STUDY 2:

(i) Read 1 Peter 1:6–12 and chapters 3 and 4 of the text.

(ii) Prayerfully consider the things that give you joy.

STUDY 2: 1 Peter 1:6–12

AIM: To appreciate the nature of our faith and to understand God's goal in guiding the process of the refinement of our faith.

1.   Why is faith the key that enables the Christian to be at peace in the midst of tribulations?

2.   How does our faith grow stronger and purer when we are distressed by various trials?

3.   Peter uses the phrase, *revelation of Jesus Christ*, rather than, *coming of Jesus Christ* in verse 7, as well as in 1:13 and 4:13. Discuss the difference between these phrases, and explain Peter's choice of phrase.

4.   Why does Peter stress that the Person and work of Christ were foretold by the prophets of the Old Testament?

5.   What is the supreme object of saving faith, and why is it vital that we exercise our faith in connection with that object?

6.   Discuss the ministry of the Holy Spirit in the writing of Scripture and in the preaching of Scripture.

7.   If we are truly exercising faith, what should be the source of our joy, and why can no lesser source provide us with inexpressible joy?

FOR STUDY 3:

(i)   Read 1 Peter 1:13–25 and chapters 5–7 of the text.

(ii)   Consider how a believer may know if he is walking according to the calling of God.

STUDY 3: 1 Peter 1:13–25

AIM: To understand those things to which God has called all believers.

1. Why is it misleading for believers to seek to minimize pain and maximize pleasure in determining the situations to which God has called them?

2. List and discuss as many things as possible that can intoxicate our spirits and render us incapable of rightly determining the things to which God has truly called us.

3. What do passages such as Romans 12: 1–2 and Colossians 3:1–4 tell us about the fixing of our hope and the cultivation of holiness?

4. Make a list of all the verses you can find that tell believers not to fear, then make a list of all the verses that indicate that a believer should fear. What does a comparison of these lists tell us about fearing man and fearing God?

5. Discuss what the fear of the Lord is, and what it is not.

6. Give reasons, and support them with references from Scripture, as to why it is impossible for one to fear God rightly while failing to love his brethren in Christ.

7. Why is it impossible for unregenerate people to love others in the way that Peter describes in verse 22?

8. How does the Word of God function in the accomplishment of regeneration?

9. Why must the regenerate continually feed upon the Word? Give Scriptures that tell what happens when we do, and when we do not, feed on the Word of God.

FOR STUDY 4:

(i) Read 1 Peter 2:1–8 and chapters 8 and 9 of the text.

(ii) Prayerfully consider the sources of spiritual nourishment and how regularly and vitally you are currently partaking of them.

STUDY 4: 1 Peter 2:1–8

AIM: To recognize those things that do, and that do not, impart spiritual vitality.

1. Why do the various factors in the circumstances of a believer not have the power to impede his spiritual growth (consider Romans 8:35–39 in this connection)?

2. Discuss how the sins of one's own heart, listed in verse 1, impede one's spiritual growth.

3. Why should those regenerated by God hunger and thirst for the Word? List some things in the private and corporate lives of God's people that tend to dull their appetite for the Word.

4. Explain why the principles of truth in Scripture, and the Person who is truth, namely Jesus Christ, are not in conflict, but rather in perfect cooperation.

5. How do the four things that Peter says about Christ in verse 4 relate to the condition of believers in the world and to their position in Christ?

6. What is your understanding of the holy priesthood into which believers are incorporated?

7. Explain why believers and unbelievers have such radically differing assessments of Christ.

FOR STUDY 5:

(i) Read 1 Peter 2:9–12 and chapters 10 and 11 of the text.

(ii) Think about the attitudes and actions that should belong to believers who know that they are chosen by God.

STUDY 5: 1 Peter 2:9–12

AIM: To understand how our duties as Christians are a consequence of what God has made us to be in Christ.

1. Consider the four descriptions Peter gives in verse 9 of the people of God. Why does the apostle repeatedly emphasize the corporate nature of those in Christ, and what significance does this emphasis have for believers in our day?

2. List and discuss several ways that the elect of God proclaim *the excellencies of God*.

3. In verse 10, Peter writes that his readers had been made the people of God and the recipients of divine mercy – matters that the world's persecution can never change or destroy. List other things that believers have received in Christ that cannot be taken from them.

4. In what sense does Peter use the term, *aliens and strangers*, in verse 11, and why is it important that we think of ourselves as such?

5. Give several examples of the fleshly lusts from which believers are to abstain, and explain how these wage war against our souls.

6. What is the connection between the regenerating work of God, and the personal purity of believers?

7. What is the connection between the personal purity of believers and their public behaviour, especially when they are amongst unbelievers?

FOR STUDY 6:

(i) Read 1 Peter 2:13–20 and chapters 12 and 13 of the text.

(ii) Think about the impact that your faith is having upon your relationships at work and in your family.

STUDY 6: 1 Peter 2:13–20

AIM: To understand how heavenly mindedness affects our earthly relationships and responsibilities.

1. Why should those who have their citizenship in heaven (*Eph.* 2:19; *Phil.* 3:20) be the best, not the worst, citizens of the kingdoms of this world?

2. Explain how the phrase, *for the Lord's sake*, modifies our submission to civil authorities.

3. Define and discuss the nature and limits of Christian freedom.

4. Read Romans 13:1–7 and list ways in which believers can demonstrate their submission to governing authorities and give honour to all men.

5. Why does the Word of God not condemn slavery clearly? What light does 1 Corinthians 7:17–24 shed on this issue?

6.   Can a person in a slave's position be made to sin by his master? Explain why or why not.

7.   What part does conscience and faith play in being submissive to an earthly master?

FOR STUDY 7:

(i)   Read 1 Peter 2:21–3:7 and chapters 14 and 15 of the text.

(ii) Think about how closely we are called to follow Christ's example of submission and suffering.

STUDY 7: 1 Peter 2:21–3: 7

AIM: To understand how our union with Christ in his sufferings conditions our sufferings in the world and our loving service in our homes.

1.   Why should knowing that God calls us to suffer encourage us in our sufferings?

2.   What comfort can we derive from the truth that Christ, the best Man ever to have lived, suffered far worse than we, who are far from the best, will ever suffer?

3.   Give scriptural reasons that support the assertion that in Christ we are safe and blessed even in our sufferings.

4.   How does faith in Christ perform the diverse tasks of enabling us to suffer resolutely and of prompting us to love our families tenderly?

5.   Why does Peter give more attention to wives than to husbands in 3:1–7?

6. What are some implications that flow from knowing, and living, the truth that we are to be subject to one another in Christ? Read Ephesians 5:21–6:9 as a help in answering this question.

FOR STUDY 8:

(i) Read 1 Peter 3:8–17 and chapters 16 and 17 of the text.

(ii) Consider how humility helps us in our sufferings.

STUDY 8: 1 Peter 3:8–17

AIM: To learn how the person who is truly submissive to the Lord thinks and acts in all situations.

1. How do the components of the submissive spirit that Peter summarizes in verse 8 work to reinforce each other?

2. What attitudes would prompt us to repay evil with evil? What good would come from acting out such attitudes?

3. Give at least three reasons why we should bless, rather than curse, those who commit evil against us. How are we to understand the imprecatory Psalms in the light of our calling to bless those who curse us?

4. What is the nature of the blessing we receive when we return good for evil?

5. Why do most people, even the ungodly, usually commend people who are zealous for good works?

6. How does being thrust into furnaces of affliction set us free from fear?

7. How do we sanctify Christ practically as Lord in our hearts?

8. God teaches us to do what is right, even if we suffer for it. Why would we feel tempted to do wrong in the midst of suffering; what do we think will be accomplished by doing wrong?

FOR STUDY 9:

(i) Read 1 Peter 3:18–22 and chapters 18 and 19 of the text.

(ii) Contemplate the relative powers of suffering and sin in their ability to injure the believer.

STUDY 9: 1 Peter 3:18–22

AIM: To have a vital and practical understanding of the relationship between sanctification and suffering.

1. Why must we clearly understand the sufferings of Christ in order to understand the divine purpose in our own sufferings?

2. List some practical comforts that come to believers through contemplating the supreme suffering of Christ, his suffering for sins, his suffering in place of those deserving it, and the blessed results of his suffering.

3. What is the clear and vital point of Christ's proclamation (verse 19), and what is its significance for us?

4. What are some similarities between the flood in Noah's day and the believers' experience of baptism?

5. According to Peter, what is the nature and saving virtue of baptism?

6. What practical consequences flow from the believer's union with Christ in his resurrection and ascension?

7. What light does Rom. 8:28 shed upon our understanding of the capacity of our enemies to harm us?

FOR STUDY 10:

(i) Read 1 Peter 4:1–11 and chapters 20 and 21 in the text.

(ii) Think about how you have profited spiritually from afflictions that you have suffered in the past.

STUDY 10: 1 Peter 4:1–11

AIM: To see the good results issuing from our suffering for our faith, and to exercise the graces that the Lord strengthens through our sufferings.

1. If Christ has suffered in the flesh for us, why must we prepare ourselves to suffer in the flesh?

2. List some specific ways in which your sufferings have served to reduce your sinning and increase your living for the Lord.

3. Describe how you have experienced the surprise of unbelieving friends over your conversion to Christ. Describe also any experience of being mocked or maligned by them.

4. Has the way you have borne your sufferings for Christ served to convict any unbelievers, leading to their conversion? If so, tell how.

5. Why is it important that believers always live with a vital awareness of the end of all things?

6.   List ways that we can pray for, and lovingly serve our brethren in Christ, even when we ourselves are under the pressure of affliction.

7.   Explain why it is right and loving for Peter to address his suffering readers, not as helpless victims but as victorious soldiers.

FOR STUDY 11:

(i)   Read 1 Peter 4:12–19 and chapters 22 and 23 in the text.

(ii) Reflect upon your characteristic response to suffering. How do you feel about the Lord, his Word, your brethren, and your enemies when you are suffering?

STUDY 11: 1 Peter 4:12–19

AIM: To recognize that there are right and wrong ways to suffer, and to learn to avoid the wrong ways while responding in right ways.

1.   Why should we be concerned more with the righteous product of our suffering than with the pain?

2.   If our sufferings do not indicate that we are cursed and cast off by God, list at least three things that they do indicate.

3.   Explain how and why we should be prepared to endure sufferings.

4.   List several wrong things for which we should not suffer, and explain why a Christian should never suffer for those things.

5.   For what should we be prepared to suffer at any cost? Why?

6. How do you feel towards your persecutors when you do not perceive the judgment of God under which they stand? What difference does your perception of the divine judgment upon them make in your attitude towards your persecutors, and therefore towards your afflictions, and your God?

FOR STUDY 12:

(i) Read 1 Peter 5:1–7 and chapters 24 and 25 in the text.

(ii) Define humility, and spend some time considering your definition.

STUDY 12: 1 Peter 5:1–7

AIM: To understand the true nature of leadership in the churches of Christ, and to know the true direction in which Christians should be led.

1. What is the true basis for service in Christ's church, and why is it essential?

2. What are the responsibilities of elders, as Peter delineates them? Are there other Scriptures which discuss these? If so, list, compare and contrast them.

3. Explain why Peter was the right man to exhort the elders to whom he wrote.

4. In what attitude should elders serve, and why is that attitude so critical?

5. Are all Christians to practise humility? If so, will the church become paralysed as all its members seek to prostrate themselves before one another? Explain why or why not.

6. Explain how we are to clothe ourselves with humility in practice.

7. Why is God opposed to the proud? Why does God exalt the humble? What determines when God will exalt the humble?

8. Explain how you can cast all your anxiety upon the Lord.

FOR STUDY 13:

(i) Read 1 Peter 5: 8–14 and read chapters 26 and 27 in the text.

(ii) Consider how aware you are of the devil and his wiles.

STUDY 13: 1 Peter 5:8–14

AIM: To understand the nature and necessity of spiritual warfare, and to learn how best to appropriate the grace of God in resisting Satan and embracing our brethren in Christ.

1. Why is there no contradiction between casting our cares upon the Lord and being carefully alert and prepared for spiritual warfare?

2. List the aspects of preparation for spiritual warfare given by Peter, and define each one, explaining why it is vital for our standing in the evil day.

3. Why is it so important that we know in some detail the nature and tactics of the devil?

4. Peter tells us that we have one effective tactic to employ against Satan. What is that tactic? Explain how it operates, and how it fits in with what Paul describes as the full armour of God (*Eph.* 6:10–18).

5. Explain why vigilance against Satan does not diminish but rather increases, tender loving regard for our brethren in Christ.

6. Discuss the implications involved in Peter's reference to Rome as Babylon.

7. Explain the connection between God's grace, our peace, and final glory.

FOR FURTHER READING

The following books are recommended for the study of 1 Peter:

J. N. D. KELLY, *The Epistles of Peter and Jude* (Black's New Testament Commentary), Peabody, MA: Hendrickson Publishers, Inc., 1999 (Originally published, A. & C. Black Ltd., London, 1969).

ROBERT LEIGHTON, *Commentary on First Peter*, Grand Rapids: Kregel Publications, 1972 (originally published in 1693).

R. C. H. LENSKI, *The Interpretation of the Epistles of St Peter, St John, and St Jude* (Commentary on the New Testament), Peabody, MA: Hendrickson Publishers, Inc., 2001.

ALEXANDER NISBET, *1 & 2 Peter* (Geneva Series of Commentaries), Edinburgh: Banner of Truth, 1982 (Originally published 1658).